"As an Early Christianity scholar, I found Dan Brown's *Da Vinci Code* (read horizontally under a spacious cedar of Lebanon, in Granada) to be one of the funniest novels I have come across in a long time. I found it bore as much relation to reality as *Raiders of the Lost Ark* did to Old Testament archaeology, or *Indiana Jones and the Last Crusade* to medieval studies. Nevertheless, when I returned from vacation, I was amazed to find some local church congregations anxiously asking me to address them and 'refute' its 'disturbing claims.'

"I have since found that the ironies of postmodern literature, which have increasingly taken historical dressage as their front, adding a dash of esoteric religion (of sorts), stirred together with liberal sloshes of conspiracy theory and anti-ecclesiastic bile, are often lost on the same readership that pantingly laps them up. If I were ever to write a novel and make some money, it would surely begin with the assassination of the Archbishop of Canterbury at the hands of the last descendant of Rameses the Second (Pharaonic material supplied courtesy of the *Scorpion King*). Meanwhile I waste my talents trying to pursue real history.

"Nancy de Flon and John Vidmar's book is (sadly) not likely to gross them the rewards of Mr. Brown (my own problem too), but it should prove to be a welcome addition to the bookshelves of anyone wishing to get a straight story; for it supplies rich and serious facts to the luminously over-the-top fiction of the *Code*. Here are some pointed scholarly questions, with sober answers delivered elegantly, accurately, and illuminating the heart of the matter. I commend both authors warmly. They make truth (almost) as interesting as fantasy."

John McGuckin
Professor of Early Christian Studies
Columbia University

101 Questions and Answers on *The Da Vinci Code* and the Catholic Tradition

101 QUESTIONS AND ANSWERS ON *THE DA VINCI CODE* AND THE CATHOLIC TRADITION

*Nancy de Flon and
John Vidmar, OP*

PAULIST PRESS
New York/Mahwah, N.J.

Cover design by Cynthia Dunne
Book design by Theresa M. Sparacio

Library of Congress Cataloging-in-Publication Data

De Flon, Nancy Marie.
    101 questions and answers on The Da Vinci code and the Catholic tradition / Nancy de Flon and John Vidmar.
        p.   cm.
    Includes bibliographical references.
    ISBN 0-8091-4412-3 (alk. paper)
    1. Brown, Dan, 1964-. Da Vinci Code. 2. Christianity in literature. I. Vidmar, John. II. Title.
PS3552.R685434D3334   2006
813'.54—dc22

                                                            2005035393

Published by Paulist Press
997 Macarthur Boulevard
Mahwah, New Jersey 07430

www.paulistpress.com

Printed and bound in the
United States of America

CONTENTS

FOREWORD

My grandma used to say, "When all you have are lemons, make lemonade."

In some ways, the phenomenal popularity of *The Da Vinci Code* has been a real "lemon" for the Catholic Church. The author beats up on her badly, pulling out old bromides, long unproven myths, and just plain inaccuracies to present the church as corrupt, oppressive, ruthless, and a liar. The sourness of this lemon is all the more bitter because the book is a real page turner, tapping into our innate human fear of, but interest in, conspiracies.

Well, thank you, Father John Vidmar, OP, and Nancy de Flon, for "making lemonade." This well-researched, eminently readable work is a godsend for all of us who have been asked for a cogent rejoinder to the best-seller. With calmness, reason, logic, and plain historical truth, our two authors have "crashed the code" and shown it to be pure fiction.

The church has long believed in "teachable moments," times in life when we are providentially open to the truth, to a deepening of faith. This book gives me hope that the popularity of *The Da Vinci Code* is indeed such a moment, when thoughtful people— Catholic or not—so perplexed by the outrageous claims of this thriller might be moved to seek "the rest of the story," and come away with a deeper respect for the church so maligned by the best-seller. So, pour a glass of lemonade, sit down, and read away.

There's nothing secretive, occult, deceptive, or hidden about *this* timely book. It's all out in the open. And "the truth shall set you free."

+ Timothy M. Dolan
Archbishop of Milwaukee

PREFACE

Anti-Catholicism appears to be one of the last remaining acceptable forms of bigotry in our politically correct society. As an attempt by a novelist to denigrate the Catholic Church under the guise of fiction, *The Da Vinci Code* represents a particularly pernicious expression of that bigotry because the author, Dan Brown, takes advantage of the fact that few people will have the knowledge necessary to be able to distinguish among truth, distortions, and downright falsehood in his 454-page thriller.

The book you have before you results from a search for the truth and for accuracy. Yet another "debunking" book? you may wonder. Well, no—because in addition to refuting Dan Brown's blatant falsehoods and inaccuracies, we also aim to present to you the richness of Catholic tradition and culture that he completely ignores. We give you Mary Magdalene as an outstanding leader in the early church and role model for us today, describe the intrigues and issues that occupied Constantine and gave rise to the Crusades, offer insights into a historian's craft, present a selection of the many women who have shaped the history of the church, and much more besides.

And we present this information in a tone that respects you, the reader. Whether you are an average Catholic in the pew or an educator seeking a resource to answer people's questions, we affirm your quest for the truth and promise that you will find our accent to be on the positive and not on all the things that Dan Brown couldn't get right.

Nancy de Flon
John Vidmar, OP

ONE

HOW HISTORY GETS WRITTEN

1. Before beginning his narrative, Dan Brown cites several "facts" and states that descriptions of art, architecture, documents, and secret rituals in his novel are accurate. Is *The Da Vinci Code* based on authentic and reliable historical sources?

On page 253, Brown's alter ego, the "Royal Historian" Sir Leigh Teabing, cites four examples from among the "scores of historians" who have allegedly "chronicled in exhaustive detail" Jesus' royal bloodline (his and Mary Magdalene's descendants). The earliest of these books, *Holy Blood, Holy Grail* (1982) by Michael Baigent et al., achieved notoriety for expanding upon the theory that Jesus and Mary Magdalene were married, that their descendants survived in France, and that because of this intimate relationship with Jesus it was actually Mary Magdalene, and not Mary the mother of Jesus, who was the object of veneration in the early church. Interestingly, you won't find information on the authors and their credentials on the book jacket. But for an indication of the level of seriousness of their research, you can note that the authors cite a book by D. Joyce titled *The Jesus Scroll* (1975), which casts doubts on Jesus' death on the cross and suggests that Barabbas—the criminal whom Pilate pardoned instead of Jesus—was Jesus' son. Not surprisingly, their bibliography lists no works by established scripture scholars.

Margaret Starbird is the author of two of the four books on Teabing's list: *The Woman with the Alabaster Jar (WAJ)* (1993) and *The Goddess in the Gospels: Reclaiming the Sacred Feminine (GG)* (1998). Both were published by Bear & Co., a publisher known chiefly for such esoteric topics as extraterrestrial consciousness, alternative medicine, and "visionary fiction." Both are highly personal rather than serious, objective attempts to research and interpret historical truth. *WAJ* is an autobiographical account of the author's personal quest for the "Lost Bride in

the Christian story," a quest continued in *GG,* in which she identifies with the Magdalene as the beloved of Jesus, whose "love is
unconditional" (p. 35).

Starbird's work depends heavily on legend (for example, a
fourth-century French legend about Mary Magdalene bringing
the "Sangraal" to southern France); on *Holy Blood, Holy Grail,*
which she cites as if it were an authoritative scholarly source;
and, in *GG,* on David Yallop's *In God's Name,* a sensationalistic
account of the alleged murder of Pope John Paul I. She discovers significance in all sorts of coincidences, such as contrived
etymologies and a contorted reading of Psalm 23 ("The Lord is
my *shepherd*"!), which she claims identifies God as feminine —
specifically, as a bride. Moreover, she discerns all kinds of
prophetic and cosmic significance in such events as the eruption
of Mount St. Helens, the Challenger disaster, and — yes — a
cracked toilet bowl, the manufacturer of which was named
Church. She also regards Tarot cards as an important source.

Starbird displays either surprising ignorance of the
Christian tradition or a readiness to distort it for her own ends.
Erroneously referring to the Virgin Mary as "the only Goddess
image allowed in Christianity" (*WAJ,* p. xxii), she also presents
an inaccurate account of the ways in which scripture was handed
down, stating that in order to be accepted into the scriptural
canon a writing had to be the authentic work of one of Jesus'
apostles. She then adds that "recent scholarship suggests" (one of
many such conveniently vague phrases she uses, all unsupported
by documentation) that none of the New Testament books is
likely to have been written by one of Jesus' apostles. Finally, she
claims that "a number of scholars consider it unlikely" that any
of the evangelists ever knew the Jesus of history. Here Starbird
has taken half kernels of fact and linked them together in such a
way as to suggest that the church is guilty of dishonesty in the
way the scriptural canon has been assembled (*WAJ,* p. 25).

This author also posits the strange notion that an understanding of Jesus as fully human is *yet to develop.* Apparently

she is (or pretends to be) unfamiliar with the writings of the church fathers, the decrees of the early ecumenical councils, such recent theologians as Karl Rahner, and a host of others in between.

Starbird's writings are seminal to the New Age concept of Mary Magdalene, and she uses her books to promote her own ideology of the danger of worshipping an "exclusively male image of God." Her claim that British Prime Minister Winston Churchill's "V for Victory" sign is the chalice (as in Holy Grail) and thus an "invocation of the Goddess" shows what a gullible readership her books are aimed at.

And yet Dan Brown considers them valid historical sources. For example, from *GG* he derived his erroneous dichotomy between a "fully human" Jesus and Jesus as the divine Son of God, as if the christological councils of Nicaea and Chalcedon had not settled this matter seventeen centuries ago (see Part Four). From *WAJ* Brown takes his cue in blaming "the church" for having portrayed Mary Magdalene for centuries as sinner and prostitute, and in maintaining that fairy tales such as Cinderella and Snow White, as well as Walt Disney's *Little Mermaid,* are associated with the theme of the Lost Bride of Jesus.

Lynn Picknett and Clive Prince, authors of *The Templar Revelation* (1997), are described as "writers, researchers, and lecturers on the paranormal, the occult, and historical and religious mysteries." Picknett has also written books on the paranormal. Their qualifications or publications as historians are not mentioned. Like the other "historical sources" already described, this one takes up the theme of blaming the church for the image of Mary Magdalene as sinner. It also appears to be the source for Brown's information on the pentagram and for the claim that the Priory of Sion serves to protect the descendants of the Merovingian royal dynasty.

2. These "scores of historians" that Teabing implies are reliable appear, then, to be bogus. In that case, how does someone

go about writing a work of history? What kinds of sources does a historian consider valid?

Historians, biographers, and other serious researchers classify their sources as primary or secondary. Primary sources include manuscripts and other original documents preserved in archives and libraries: letters, diaries, deeds, and other pertinent public and private documents. Maps and other visuals, such as drawings or possibly photographs, may also be included in primary sources. Secondary sources may consist of edited, printed collections of primary material: for example, the letters and/or journals of a particular individual, maps of a particular place, and so on. They may also include other works based on primary material as well as on other authentic secondary material.

As an example, let's take the source material on which historian David McCullough based his history of the American Revolution, *1776*. In the bibliography McCullough groups his sources into six categories. "Manuscript Collections" lists the libraries, archives, and historical societies that hold certain manuscripts and other primary source material; these include (among many others) the Colonial Williamsburg Reference Library in Virginia, the National Archives in Washington, DC, and the New-York Historical Society. "Books" contains edited collections of primary source material, such as W. W. Abbott's edition of *The Papers of George Washington* and Paul Langford's *The Writings and Speeches of Edmund Burke*. Also, since no scholar has time to "reinvent the wheel" by thoroughly checking every known primary source, this category also contains books of various aspects of history that are reliable because based on primary sources: for example, S. A. Drake's biography of *General Israel Putnam: The Commander at Bunker Hill*.

No book like McCullough's could be written without consulting "Reference Works," and this category lists such material as dictionaries, encyclopedias, and atlases. "Diaries, Journals, and Memoirs" is just that: either originally published or later editions of firsthand accounts written by participants in or eyewitnesses to

Revolutionary War events. The material in "Articles" is similar to that in "Books" but on a smaller scale. Finally, "Newspapers and Journals" date from the time of the action and thus provide contemporary news accounts.

You may be wondering whether Tarot cards could ever be considered valid source material for a work of history. Yes, they can—if you are writing about the history or iconography of Tarot cards!

3. How, then, does the historian approach and treat his or her material?

To research and write history is to be motivated by a desire to find the truth. Approaching one's task with the a priori intention of shoehorning one's findings into a preconceived agenda or ideology—and, in the process, knowingly treating spurious sources as if they were on the same level as valid sources—is not scholarship; it's intellectual dishonesty.

Note that "agenda/ideology" and "point of view" or "perspective" are two very different things. The recounting of any given event will differ depending on the point of view of each participant; for example, accounts of a Thanksgiving dinner gathering will differ according to whether the narrator is the host or hostess, another member of the host household, or an outside guest. Similarly, the story of a historical event like the American Revolution can be told from the perspective of the American generals, the British generals, or the common soldier. It can be a political history, an economic history, or a social history. The contemporary trend is, in fact, "social history"—that is, for history to be investigated and interpreted from the perspective of the ordinary person rather than along the lines of the "Great Men" or "Great Ideas" approach; that's why history told from women's point of view, or that of African Americans, is increasingly popular (and, incidentally, makes Teabing's claim on p. 256 that history is "always" written by the winners and "always" one-sided look ridiculous).

For example, a history of the Protestant Reformation may trace the development of the thought of the major Reformers such as Luther or Calvin, or analyze how such factors as town government or the printing press helped to advance the Reformation, or explore its effects on women. Regardless of these differing perspectives, all of which are valid, the story must be told by searching out and assembling the facts and then interpreting them in a spirit of humility and openness—not according to an agenda. Even a responsible author of historical fiction will base his or her work on *valid* historical writings.

The novel refers to a draft manuscript of Langdon's entitled *Symbols of the Lost Sacred Feminine* in which he offers "unconventional" and "controversial" interpretations of religious iconography (p. 24). "Unconventional" and "controversial" interpretations of one's research are nothing unusual in the academic world—but a bona fide scholar proposing such interpretations will provide firm support and documentation for them from the primary and secondary source material.

4. So, we've established that Brown's sources are, despite his claims, not bona fide works of history. But what about *The Da Vinci Code* itself? Brown was writing a novel. How does it qualify as a historical novel?

To explain this, we can distinguish among different types of fiction: historical fiction, historical romance, and detective fiction. Historical fiction is the attempt, through the use of characters and dialogue, both fictional and nonfictional, to reproduce the *feeling* of actual history, to give the reader a sense of what it was like to live in a particular age, to share in the experience of real historical figures. The reproduction of real history is the goal. Faithfulness to the facts is key. Every device is subordinated to the retelling of authentic history. A recent example of good historical fiction is Michael Shaara's Pulitzer Prize–winning *Killer Angels*. Shaara's goal was to retell a story that actually happened: the story of the battle of Gettysburg. Diaries, battle reports, memoirs were all combed to put together a picture of what the actual characters might have said or thought as the battle unfolded. We know from several sources that General Robert E. Lee was disappointed in his cavalry commander, J. E. B. Stuart, and that when Stuart finally arrived back in the Confederate lines, after missing the first two days of the battle due to his flamboyant and reckless ride around the Union army, Lee dressed him down. The author simply needed to give this some flesh, and so by creating dialogue based on these sources he put into Lee's mouth what Lee probably said.

5. What's the difference between historical fiction and historical romance?

Historical romance is the use of history as background to tell a story. The story, not the history, is important here. Margaret Mitchell's novel *Gone with the Wind* is a good example. It's the story of the relationship between Rhett Butler and Scarlett O'Hara, and Civil War Atlanta is the background for the development of their relationship. John Jakes's *North and South* is even more obviously a romance—a soap opera whose background happens to be the Civil War. The story of the Civil War is far less important than that of the lives of the people in the book. They could be placed anywhere. The background supplies only the color, so that the facts are unimportant.

This is not to say that historical romance is inferior or somehow deceitful. There are times when the historical setting determines the behavior and attitudes of the characters, and their development as characters is best set in a particular historical environment. The point is that the author of a historical romance is more concerned with the romance than with the history. And the reader clearly sees that the historical background is secondary.

6. In Brown's novel the details of various crimes are being investigated. Does *The Da Vinci Code* qualify, then, as detective fiction?

Detective fiction can fall somewhere in between historical fiction and historical romance. In most detective fiction the *puzzle* and often the *tension* are what drive the novel. The Brother Cadfael series does not really shed much light on medieval life, though it did provide the mysteries with a certain charm. In the stories and novels featuring Conan Doyle's Sherlock Holmes, G. K. Chesterton's Father Brown, Dorothy Sayers's Peter Wimsey, or Anne Perry's William Monk, the background is always interesting and colorful, but relatively unimportant compared to the detective's particular method of solving crimes. *The Hound of the Baskervilles* needs a moor, but the book is not about the moor, it is about a murder.

Dan Brown's *Da Vinci Code* tries to combine historical fiction with detective fiction. It is a typical detective novel in that there is a puzzle to be solved and a certain amount of tension in the chase. *The Da Vinci Code* wants to be like the movie *Raiders of the Lost Ark,* but with credentials and scholarship. And the author achieves this by the simple expedient of saying on an introductory page, "All descriptions of artwork, architecture, documents, and secret rituals in this novel are true." Well, yes, there *is* a Rosslyn Chapel in Scotland, and yes, Leonardo da Vinci *did* paint *The Last Supper,* but Dan Brown is saying much more than that in his book. Here is a presentation of history that is more than just color and background. As in Umberto Eco's popular novel *The Name of the Rose,* which was also unduly critical of monasticism and the medieval church, there seems to be a greater purpose at work. To some extent, the history drives the puzzle. If the history is accurate, as in good historical fiction, so much the better for the puzzle.

The problem with *The Da Vinci Code* is that the history presented by the author is not accurate. It is not only *sometimes* inaccurate, it is almost *always* inaccurate. And it is inaccurate in more than history: its descriptions of art, classical mythology, theology, church history, and biblical interpretation are all seriously flawed. The author, in fact, combines these inaccuracies in an amazing pastiche and somehow (because readers do not know the disciplines) convinces the reader that he is onto something. One author (Richard Barber: *The Holy Grail: Imagination and Belief,* 2004) observes that this appears to be a new genre at work, which he calls "fictional history." We might say it's the writing of pure, made-up fiction in such a way as to convince people or fool them into thinking that it's authentic history. Unfortunately, "fictional history" is precisely what we're dealing with in *The Da Vinci Code.*

What disappoints the reader who knows anything about any of the disciplines that Dan Brown touches on in *The Da Vinci Code* is the shoddiness of the research, the inaccuracy of the so-called "facts" listed, and the ludicrousness of the connections made. This is not how history, historical fiction, or even detective fiction gets written by reputable authors who take their craft seriously.

Two

The New Testament

7. Dan Brown claims that the Emperor Constantine commissioned a new Bible (p. 231; see also Q. 25). How, actually, did the Bible take its final form?

If Dan Brown were correct, this would mean that not until the year 325 or later did the Christian church have an accepted body of writings. In fact, before the end of the second century, the four gospel accounts and the thirteen letters written by or attributed to St. Paul were generally accepted by the church as "canonical," or approved, by the Christian community itself. Christians wanted to hear the earliest and best accounts of the life of Christ and Paul's words of wisdom on Christian living.

An important motivation for the church's deciding on a formally accepted body of sacred writings was that by the year 180 new writings were appearing that tried to mimic the earlier writings while injecting false teachings. Among them were the Gnostic Gospels (see Q. 15). In coming to grips with Gnostic writings and other factors, the church was faced with its earliest issue of authority. The original generation of apostles and other witnesses had died out, leaving an open field for the spread of false teachings. The church needed to establish continuity with the original apostolic witness to the truth. Two ways in which the church responded to this challenge were the establishment of people in administrative and pastoral functions (bishops, presbyters, deacons) and the formulation of creeds, or formal articulations of faith. The Nicene Creed, which we commonly use today, wasn't formulated until the fourth century (see Q. 26). In the meantime, however, baptismal confessions of faith served the purpose. These were not officially composed forms but rather evolved first in an informal way as oral tradition. A third way in which the church responded to challenges to authentic teaching was to decide on a canonical body of sacred texts.

8. How did the formation of the New Testament canon help protect the church's authority?

The formation of authoritative scriptural writings, or what we call today the New Testament canon, was begun in the second century and finalized in the fourth century. It was spurred by a growing recognition that such an authorized collection of writings was needed, especially where the teachings of Jesus were concerned; and it involved a process by which certain Christian writings were acknowledged to have the same essential place in the church as the Hebrew Scriptures, so that they came to be regarded as having been inspired by the Holy Spirit. Many writings never made it into the canon; some of them we refer to as the apocryphal writings (see Q. 17).

Three criteria were required for a writing to be accepted as canonical:

First, a work had to be reasonably regarded as written by an apostle or some other contemporary witness.

Second, it had to be considered orthodox in its teaching, that is, regarded as reflecting the authentic beliefs of the early Christians. Interestingly, some people opposed including the Gospel of John because the Gnostics held it in high esteem, as did the followers of a heretic named Montanus; but it was very widely used and had the name of an apostle associated with it. Later, when the canon was being finalized, the three "Letters of John" were included because, in opposition to some members of the Johannine community (see Q. 12) who wanted to exaggerate John's Gospel's focus on Jesus' divinity, these letters are intent on stressing his humanity.

Third, the writing had to have antiquity on its side: it had to be continuous with the earliest Christian tradition, not a later writing or something claimed to have been "lost and rediscovered."

The process of recognizing approved texts was a way of protecting the faithful from false teachers who appeared to be Christians but who were trying to spread a message at considerable variance to the Gospel of Jesus Christ. Approved texts were also a way of telling Christians that they were a united community and that they could not go off on their own and believe what they wanted about Jesus Christ. It is striking how early on Christianity became affected by erroneous teachings, yet perhaps not surprising given the inevitability of its coming into contact with the plethora of belief systems prevalent in the Roman Empire.

9. How did the four gospel accounts originate?

The memories of those who knew Christ personally—especially the twelve apostles because they had been with Christ from the start—were shared in early Christian liturgies, at first through the oral transmission of stories from one person to another. Eventually, however, these early eyewitnesses began to die off, and certain Christians began to record these stories in writing. They gave the stories a certain shape, adapting them to the circumstances of their audience, much as preachers or speakers do today.

We can state with reasonable certainty that, besides these gospel accounts, there are no other documents about the life of Christ dating from this same time. Noted scripture scholar John Meier has stated that there is no better, contemporary evidence for the life of Christ than the four gospel accounts. They are the earliest, written within the lifetime of people who knew Christ personally.

10. It sounds as if the four Gospels have been around much longer than Dan Brown claims. Did the Gospel writers know Jesus personally?

The authors are traditionally known as Matthew, Mark, Luke, and John. For many centuries Matthew and John were identified as two of the twelve apostles, and Mark and Luke as two companions of apostles mentioned in the Acts of the Apostles. Biblical scholarship over the last two hundred years, however, has cast doubt on and even disproved these authorships. In New Testament times a practice called *pseudonymity* was common, in which a name was attached to a piece of writing in order to confirm its validity and seal its authenticity, just as was done with the Hebrew Scriptures, in which the Pentateuch (the first five books) was traditionally attributed to Moses. Although the Gospel was not actually written by that person, in some cases it may have originated in a tradition associated with him.

11. In that case, who were Matthew, Mark, Luke, and John, and how did each of them come to write the Gospel named after him?

A second-century source suggests that the apostle Matthew may have begun the tradition that led to the writing of the Gospel that bears his name by collecting the sayings of Jesus. You will notice that this Gospel concentrates heavily on Jesus' teachings, such as the Sermons on the Mount and the parables. The real author, however, is unknown. His audience was comprised largely of Jewish Christians, and most scholars believe that the author was one, too. Intent upon showing that the prophecies in the Hebrew Scriptures were being fulfilled in Christ, Matthew's Gospel is significant in its linking of Judaism with early Christianity. It was probably written between AD 80 and 90.

Although the early fathers of the church identified the author of the Gospel of Mark as John Mark, the companion of Paul mentioned in the New Testament (Col 4:10, Acts 12:25), we do not know for certain who the author was, though it could possibly have been this person. The Gospel was likely written in Rome in the 60s AD for a community threatened with persecution or already being persecuted. Internal evidence—that is, the actual content of a Gospel—helps scripture scholars determine such matters as when, where, and for whom it was written. While we believe that the Holy Spirit inspired the writing of the sacred scriptures, this does not mean that they were written in a vacuum, unaffected by historical circumstances.

Scholars are divided about the authorship of Luke's Gospel. Written about AD 90, it has been attributed to a companion of Paul mentioned in the New Testament. The author never identifies himself, however. Possibly this Gospel was written in Antioch, the third-largest city in the Roman Empire and an important center for the growing Gentile church. Luke's Gospel is actually the first part of a two-volume set. The second volume is the Acts of the Apostles, written by the same author as an account of the earliest Christian communities.

The next question addresses the authorship of the Gospel of John.

12. What are the "Synoptic Gospels"? And how does the Gospel of John fit in?

The Gospels of Matthew, Mark, and Luke are called the "Synoptic" Gospels, from the Greek words meaning "to see together," because these three Gospels are very similar in their presentation of Jesus' life and ministry. They tend to present the same events, the same miracles, sometimes even word for word.

The Gospel of John, however, differs markedly from the Synoptics. It recounts stories of Jesus' miracles—John calls them "signs"—not found in the Synoptic Gospels, such as the changing of water into wine at the wedding at Cana and the raising of Lazarus. Unlike the Synoptics, it does not tell of Jesus instituting the Eucharist at the Last Supper, but instead it depicts him washing the disciples' feet as an example of the service expected of them. John's Gospel is not so much an account of Jesus as a theological reflection on him, and it focuses on Jesus as the incarnate Word of God who existed from all time. The last of the four canonical Gospels to be written, the Gospel of John dates from around AD 100 and was probably written at Ephesus. It traces its origins to the "beloved disciple," otherwise unnamed, who may have been the original editor of the material and who, until the eighteenth century, was erroneously identified as John the apostle, son of Zebedee. In its final form this sublime Gospel is the work not of one person but of a group of early Christians known as the Johannine community, or community of John.

13. In what order were the Gospels written?

From the time of St. Augustine in the fifth century until the nineteenth century the "traditional" order—Matthew, Mark, Luke, and John—was believed to be correct. But then scholars, noting that Mark seemed to be a primary source for Matthew and Luke, became convinced that Mark actually came first. Thus the "two-source theory" was formulated, which postulates that Matthew's primary sources were Mark and "Q."

14. What is the "Q" document? In the novel, Leigh Teabing hints that it contains a secret teaching about Christ that is at odds with Christian orthodoxy (p. 256).

"Q" comes from the German word *Quelle*, meaning "source." A nineteenth-century scholar put forth the theory that Matthew and Luke borrowed from a core body of material that preserved the sayings of Jesus and was shared by the Christian community. This theory is meant to explain the source from which Matthew and Luke derived material shared by them but not found in Mark. The existence of a "Q" source is widely accepted today, although it is not a "document," despite what Teabing claims, and may even have been an oral rather than written source (see Q. 7).

THREE

GNOSTICISM

15. What are the Gnostic Gospels? Leigh Teabing possesses a huge leather-bound book that he describes as photocopies of the Nag Hammadi and Dead Sea Scrolls (p. 245), which supposedly contain these documents.

First, the Nag Hammadi Library and the Dead Sea Scrolls are two *very* different things. The Dead Sea Scrolls were discovered in 1947 in caves near the Dead Sea at Qumran and are thought to have been the library of the Essenes, a Jewish sect that may well have influenced John the Baptist. Among these scrolls are many of the books in the Hebrew Scriptures. Because they date from the first century BC, they are considerably older than any other of those texts that are still extant.

The Nag Hammadi Library consists of thirteen codices that were discovered in 1945 in Egypt, near a fourth-century monastery. These writings originated with those who espoused and taught Gnosticism. This discovery has been invaluable in shedding light on the tenets of Gnosticism, which was by no means a homogenous belief system.

Brown's allusion to a huge bound book of photocopies wrongly (and no doubt intentionally) implies that these texts are secret and only accessible to specialist scholars. In fact, both the Dead Sea Scrolls and the Nag Hammadi Library are readily available in English translation to anyone who wishes to go to their local bookstore and buy a paperback copy—or to borrow one from their public library.

16. Who were the Gnostics?

When Christianity spread to the wider world—the Diaspora, Hellenistic Jews, and Gentiles—it encountered a very different mentality from that of Jewish Palestine. Some of the people who came into contact with and embraced Christianity were uncomfortable with the notion of a tangible God—one who "pitched his tent" among us as a human being—and would have preferred that the Christian news expressed itself in the realm of timeless myth rather than in the story of a real human being born of a woman. This is how Christianity came to have one of its first experiences of heresy— specifically, the heresy of Gnosticism.

Gnosticism existed before Christianity and so isn't intrinsically a Christian movement. Some persons who sympathized with the Gnostic mind-set became Christians and tried to adapt the Christian message to Gnostic thinking. Gnosticism was, however, by no means a monolithic system of beliefs or action.

The word *Gnostic* comes from the Greek word *gnosis,* meaning "knowledge." Gnostics regarded themselves as an elite body of people, an in-group with special knowledge that ordinary believers didn't have. This knowledge concerned how the world originated, and how evil came about, and how a person could be delivered from evil.

The most famous Christian Gnostic teacher, Marcion, who lived in the second century, rejected the Hebrew Scriptures because, as he saw it, the god of the Old Testament is an angry, punishing God, not at all the same as the New Testament God of love that Jesus proclaimed. Marcion taught that the material world was created not by the supreme good God—the Father of Jesus Christ— but by the inferior Old Testament god whom he called a *demiurge.* Thus it followed that the Gnostics came to regard the physical world as evil. If matter was evil, God could not truly have become incarnate. The incarnation then is an illusion; Christ only *appeared* to be human. This thinking led to the early heresy of Docetism, the teaching that Jesus only went through the motions of being human—and of suffering and dying. Consistent with his low view of the material world, Marcion forbade his followers to engage in sexual intercourse, even in marriage. In the history of Christianity, Gnosticism was an early factor that provided an impetus for defining orthodoxy and asking and settling certain questions of teaching and discipline (see Q. 7).

17. Are the Gnostic Gospels authentic Christian writings?

The Gnostic Gospels belong to a body of Christian literature called the "apocryphal writings." Apocryphal writings took many forms, such as "Acts," like the biblical Acts of the Apostles, except that they focused on one person, like St. Peter or St. Paul. Some information that has entered the realm of popular belief, but is not corroborated in scripture, comes from these writings; for example, the *Acts of Peter* tells how St. Peter was crucified upside down.

Another form was the Infancy Gospel, of which the most famous are the *Protoevangelium of James* and the *Infancy Gospel of Thomas*. These purport to record events of Jesus' childhood years and include such pious legends as one about little Jesus miraculously turning clay birds into real ones.

There is nothing "secret" about the apocryphal writings. They have been thoroughly studied by scripture scholars and are readily available in translation. There are no "hidden," suppressed documents. *Excluding* a text from the scriptural canon is not the same thing as *suppressing* it altogether. In fact, some apocryphal material is so widely known as to be considered in the popular mind as orthodox. An example is the story of Veronica wiping the face of Jesus with her veil, long familiar not only in the Stations of the Cross, but also, more recently, through the Shroud of Turin, for which some claim connection to that story.

18. Why did the church reject these writings?

Writings such as these were rejected from the church's scriptural canon for various reasons. With the passing of time, some of the stories were realized to be little more than pious legend, as with the Infancy Gospels. More seriously, some were rejected because of their false teachings; for example, in its account of the crucifixion of Jesus the *Gospel of Peter* suggests that Jesus was not truly human because he did not appear to suffer. From an early time, as we have seen (see Q. 16), the church had to contend against the heresy of Docetism, and ensuring that such writings were kept out of the mainstream of Christian thought was essential to this. So, it's quite ironic that Brown insists on accusing the early church of trying to promote Christ's divinity at the expense of his humanity, and on claiming that the texts he champions—the Gnostic texts—are the true ones, since these are precisely the ones that reject Jesus' humanity.

These writings were not excluded because the church needed to hide a secret. Here Brown, like the authors of *Holy Blood, Holy Grail* and other spurious sources on which he bases his novel, is buying into the "conspiracy theory of history" much in vogue today (the many hypotheses surrounding John F. Kennedy's assassination are a good example). In fact, translations of most of these writings are readily available for purchase or borrowing from libraries.

19. Are the Gnostic Gospels the earliest Christian records, as Teabing says (p. 245)?

Quite the opposite. The canonical Gospels (the four Gospels accepted into the NT), which Brown claims were commissioned by Constantine in the fourth century, predate the Gnostic and other apocryphal writings, sometimes by centuries. We have seen that the four New Testament Gospels were written before the end of the first century AD (see QQ. 11, 12). The formation of the New Testament canon began at least as early as the middle of the second century, when the church was spurred to define what was authentic by the appearance of writings that contained false teachings (see Q. 7). In fact, while discussion continued until the fourth century over the canonicity of some of the letters and the Book of Revelation, there was never a question about the four Gospels or about including any other Gospel in the Bible.

The two Gnostic Gospels that Brown treats as containing authentic, suppressed teachings—the *Gospel of Philip* and the *Gospel of Mary*—are from the late third and the fifth centuries, respectively. The only apocryphal gospel that any scholar takes seriously at all is the *Gospel of Thomas,* a Coptic writing containing 114 sayings attributed to Jesus, of which about one third have approximate parallels in the canonical Gospels. But Brown never references this one at all!

20. Is Brown correct in saying that the Gnostic Gospels don't match up with the canonical Gospels?

To a great extent, yes. We have just seen that the Gnostic Gospels were written later than the canonical Gospels. As with any record, the further removed in time one gets from the events, the more likely it is that errors will creep in. Recall what we said about historical research (see Q. 2): to be reliable, it must be based on primary sources that date from the same time as, or as close as possible to the time of, the actual event or person being researched. To be sure, the evangelists weren't writing "histories" as we use the term today, but they were recording, each for the specific needs of his own community, the good news about Jesus, God incarnate who came to earth, died, and rose again, and we have seen the importance the early church placed on *witness,* on the testimony of those who actually walked with Jesus or who knew those who did.

Further, it was not the writers of the canonical Gospels—who sought to preserve the truth about Jesus—but the Gnostics who were promoting their own agenda. This, plus the distance in time from the events they purport to record, would have given rise to the errors they contain and thus led to their rejection by the church.

FOUR

_____

CONSTANTINE AND CHRISTIANITY
IN THE ROMAN EMPIRE

21. The Roman Emperor Constantine (ca. 274–337) is blamed in the novel for many alleged "misdeeds" of the Catholic Church. How much of what Brown says about Constantine is true? For example, did he really become a Christian only on his deathbed?

Let's take this one issue at a time. First, the "Royal Historian" Teabing implies that the official religion of the Roman Empire was sun worship and that Constantine shunted it aside in favor of Christianity. He also says that Constantine remained a pagan all his life and was baptized only on his deathbed, against his will (p. 232).

Sun worship—the cult of *Sol Invictus,* or the Unconquered Sun—was one of many forms of Roman religion, and at one point in his life Constantine espoused this cult. This is hardly surprising, since Constantine was a soldier and this cult was very popular among the military; however, sun worship was not the official, exclusive form of religion in the empire (see Q. 27). Incidentally, this statement of Teabing's conflicts with other claims made throughout the novel that Roman religion was exclusively about goddess worship!

Constantine's favorable attitude toward Christianity stems from his famous victory over his rival coemperor at the Milvian Bridge. He fought this battle after being inspired in a dream or vision to have his soldiers paint the Christian Chi-Rho monogram ☧ on their shields. Yet, it is unclear precisely when or to what extent he began to consider himself a Christian. He was not baptized until just before he died, that much is true (*Da Vinci,* p. 232); but this was not an uncommon procedure in those days. Christians believed that baptism forgave the sins one had committed up to then, but as yet there was no developed concept of the sacrament of penance as we now know it; thus people were

31

uncertain about how or whether sins committed post-baptism could be forgiven. And so many people who considered themselves Christians did not actually receive baptism until "the last minute." Thus, the fact that Constantine was baptized on his deathbed does not mean that he officially remained and worshipped as a pagan for his entire life.

22. Did Constantine forcibly convert the Roman Empire from pagan to Christian in the year 325, as the novel suggests?

In a word, no. Constantine achieved his military victory in 312. In 313 he and his coemperor in the East, Licinius, issued the Edict of Milan, which granted Christians full legal rights alongside other religions in the Empire. Constantine—who, like his father, the Emperor Constantius, had always opposed the persecution of Christians—was grateful to the Christian God for favoring him in battle, and he was astute enough to realize the potential that a monotheistic religion like Christianity had for bringing stability to the empire. It was *not* a matter of "warring pagans and Christians" needing to be brought into line, as Dan Brown suggests (p. 232). The Edict of Milan also ordered all church property that had been confiscated during the persecutions to be restored.

23. I've heard it said that Constantine made Christianity the official religion of the Roman Empire. Is this true?

No. The Edict of Milan decreed that Christianity had an equal right to be tolerated along with the other religions in the empire. Christianity didn't become the official religion until 380, when Emperor Theodosius decreed that all people of the empire should profess the Christian faith. Constantine did, however, give individual churches monetary gifts for charitable purposes and, at his own expense, had basilicas erected for Christian worship. For example, he was responsible for building the basilica on the site of the Holy Sepulchre at Jerusalem and, at Constantinople, the original Hagia Sophia (church dedicated to Holy Wisdom).

In 321 Constantine decreed that Sunday, the Christian day of worship, would be a weekly holiday from work. Note that Sunday was already the Christian holy day: the statement in Brown's novel (p. 232)—that Christians kept the Jewish Sabbath of Saturday until Constantine shifted it to coincide with the pagan Day of the Sun— is false. Already in the New Testament (Acts 20:7 and 1 Cor 16:2) we read of the Christian practice of assembling on Sunday, the first day of the week. The early Christians also called Sunday the Lord's Day, because it was the day of the Lord's resurrection. On this day they assembled for a ritual meal and eucharistic worship, although by the time of Justin Martyr in the second century the Eucharist had become a separate rite independent of the communal meal.

24. When did Christians begin to regard Jesus as divine?

According to Dan Brown, until the time of Constantine Christians held Jesus to be no more than an ordinary, mortal prophet, albeit a great man, and the notion of Jesus' divinity was first proposed and decided upon at Nicaea (p. 233). This is not true. That Jesus was viewed as divine from a very early stage—in fact, from within a few years of his death—is already clear from the four Gospels, which were written in the first century. In fact, the gospel writers coped with the challenge of delicately balancing Jesus' humanity with the qualities that showed his very special connection to God. A good example is the nature of Jesus' knowledge: Did he possess the limited knowledge normal to humans or extraordinary knowledge that suggests he was divine? The Gospels show both. For example, in Mark (5:30–33), when an ailing woman touches Jesus' garments in hopes of being healed, he asks, "Who touched my clothes?" Thus, he appears to have had ordinary, limited human knowledge. Yet, in John's Gospel, which tends to portray Jesus without human weakness, Jesus foretells that Judas will betray him (6:71, 13:11).

Jesus' miracles are often regarded as demonstrating his divinity. Scripture scholar Father Raymond Brown points out that to understand the real significance of the miracles we must view them not as deeds performed to evoke astonishment (as the English word *miracle* would suggest) but as "acts of power" (as the Greek word *dynamis* suggests), which is the description most commonly used of them in the Synoptic Gospels. Jesus used these acts of power as a means of reclaiming the world from the thrall of Satan. In distinction from the miracles performed by such Old Testament prophets as Elijah, Jesus' acts—or "signs," as John's Gospel calls them—are associated with the inbreaking of God's kingdom. Raymond Brown observes, "Jesus by his actions clearly presents himself as changing the governance of the world and of human lives" (*An Introduction to New Testament Christology,* p. 65). Jesus introduces God's kingdom in such a way as to suggest strongly that he is to be identified with God.

The Gospels present testimony about Jesus' divinity. At his baptism in the River Jordan, and again at his transfiguration, a voice from heaven, understood to be that of God the Father, proclaims, "This is my Son, the Beloved" (Matt 3:17, 17:5; Mark 9:7; Luke 9:35). In Matthew's and Mark's Gospels the centurion who witnessed Jesus' death exclaimed, "Truly this was the Son of God!" (Matt 27:54; Mark 15:39). And in John's Gospel, when St. Thomas encounters the risen Jesus, he says, "My Lord and my God!" (John 20:28). Whether or not these people actually said these things doesn't matter: the point is that the inclusion of these stories in the Gospels shows that the Christian communities for which these Gospels were written already believed Jesus to be divine. So while the early Christians of course knew Jesus to be a human being, they also recognized his divinity: he was the Son of God.

25. You say the New Testament shows that the early Christians regarded Jesus as the Son of God. But doesn't Dan Brown say that Constantine ordered the Bible to be rewritten to prove Jesus' divinity (p. 234)?

Quite simply, the answer is no. None of the writings in the New Testament was written later than the early second century, while Constantine lived in the fourth century. The "suppressed gospels" that Brown would like to claim as the "authentic" early Christian writings were actually written later, sometimes considerably later (see Q. 19).

By claiming (wrongly) that Constantine had to rewrite history by suppressing gospels that recorded Jesus' human traits and accentuating gospels that portrayed him as divine, Brown constructs a false dichotomy between Jesus' humanity and his divinity. Christianity holds that Jesus is fully divine and fully human: "true God *and* true man," not one *or* the other. And the supposedly "rewritten" Gospels in the canonical New Testament certainly present Jesus as a human being as normal as you or me.

Jesus is shown as compassionate, as evidenced by the number of times he heals people (e.g., Matt 8:1–4, 9:20–22, 9:36, 14:14, 15:32; Mark 1:32–34, 40–42; 8:1–8; Luke 5:12–13, 7:11–15). We see him enjoying people's company at social gatherings (e.g., Mark 2:15; Luke 5:29, 10:38–42; John 12:1–2). Jesus becomes angry, for example when he turns the commercial interests out of the Temple (Matt 21:12–13; Mark 11:15–17; Luke 19:45, 46; John 2:13–16), and when he curses the fig tree because it is barren and he is hungry (Matt 21:18–19; Mark 11:12–14). He weeps — over Jerusalem for its lack of faith (Luke 19:41–42) and at the death of his friend Lazarus (John 11:35). He becomes tired and thirsty (John 4:6–7). Gospel writers anxious to play down the humanity of Jesus would hardly have included events such as these.

One could not possibly think otherwise than that the concept of Jesus as truly human, as defined by the Council of Chalcedon in 451, is of vital importance to Christian faith! As Raymond Brown points out, how else could we grasp the depth of God's love for us? In Jesus, the second Person of the Trinity became a fully human being subject to all our human weaknesses except sin, a man who saw his future and the horror of his fate gradually unfolding in front of him. A Jesus who simply walked through earthly life as if playing a part and speaking a prearranged script would hardly have been a Savior with whom we could identify or who could give us hope. If Jesus' death has any meaning for us, it's because it was as agonizing as any human death can be.

26. So, what was the Council of Nicaea? And what did the bishops agree on at the council?

Dan Brown gives no date for the Council of Nicaea, but *this* was the great event that occurred in 325, the year when he claims Constantine decided to unify the empire under the Christian banner and stamp out paganism. Nicaea was the first of the twenty-one ecumenical councils of the church.

The Council of Nicaea was convened because a presbyter named Arius contended that the Logos or Word of God, whom we identify as the Second Person of the Blessed Trinity who became incarnate in Jesus, was a creature and did not exist from all eternity. Arius was prominent and popular and his views spread quickly, so that not only churchmen but the entire populace became caught up in the controversy. Everyone seemed to have a strong opinion on it, much as Americans today might strongly favor one baseball team over another in the World Series. The empire stood to be divided over this issue.

Consequently, Constantine summoned all the bishops in the empire to the city of Nicaea and insisted that they resolve this issue. He didn't care *how* they resolved it, as long as they agreed on something: Was the Logos equal with God (divine) or was he merely a creature? Constantine was concerned for the unity of the empire, but it wasn't a matter of ending wars between pagans and Christians, as Brown would have us believe, but of resolving a theological dispute among Christians.

After much discussion, the bishops absolutely rejected Arius's position that the Logos is a creature. They held that the Logos, or Word of God, is divine, just as is the Father. The phrases the bishops used—"true God from true God," "begotten not made," "one in substance [Being] with the Father"—are the same as we say today about the Lord Jesus in the Nicene

Creed. The opposing position has gone down in history as the Arian heresy.

Brown's assertion that those who chose the supposed "gospels" accentuating Jesus' humanity over Constantine's "new version" that made Jesus divine were the first heretics (p. 234) is false. Heresies had arisen in the church as early as the first century; many of them were connected with Gnostic teachings (see Section Three). Historically, heresy was always defined in reaction to a threat against accepted tradition. Heretics actually challenged the church to define beliefs that had traditionally been taken for granted. It's as if someone were challenging an accepted family tradition by proposing, "Let's open our presents on Christmas eve." "But," comes the answer, "we always open them on Christmas morning." Opening the presents on Christmas morning wasn't a predetermined rule; it was a gradually established tradition, and only the suggestion to change caused the tradition to be formally expressed in words.

One must keep in mind that in the early centuries of Christianity the understanding of Jesus' nature underwent a gradual development; it wasn't a matter of one person or group suddenly discarding what had been held previously in order to effect a change. What was important to St. Athanasius, the bishop of Alexandria who led the opposition to Arius at Nicaea, was that the Nicene statement of faith be "loyal to the direction of the NT" (Raymond Brown, *New Testament Christology,* p. 143). Raymond Brown quotes Athanasius as saying, "If the expressions are not in so many words in the Scriptures, yet they contain the sense of the Scriptures" (ibid., p. 143). As Father Brown states elsewhere in his book, in early Christianity we are speaking of "a development during the first century that involves a growing Christian understanding about the identity of Jesus, not the creation ex nihilo of a new identity" (p. 109).

27. Did Constantine deliberately stamp out the goddess religion and replace it with Christianity?

Dan Brown's suggestion (e.g., pp. 46, 248) of a monolithic pre-Christian goddess religion that was forcibly suppressed in favor of Christianity is erroneous. Roman religion, for example, was multilayered, not monolithic. The public or state religion was closely connected with patriotism. In *The World of Rome,* historian Michael Grant (a *real, bona fide* historian) points to the wide empire's belief that Rome's prosperity "depended on proper ritual performances and on the upkeep of the national holy places." Romans in the empire worshipped its deceased emperors as deities. Privately, every family worshipped its own household deities, or *lares*—a rough equivalent would be Catholic patron saints.

By the time of Constantine, several different cults had sprung up as people sought hope against a universal belief in fate or chance, an oppressive mind-set to which religion could offer no answer. There was a growing hope for a next world; savior deities—many of whom were believed to have died and risen again—became very popular in the Mediterranean region as people increasingly sought spiritual salvation.

One exceedingly popular and widespread cult was that of the Persian sun god Mithras, the *Sol Invictus,* regarded as a mediator between divinity and humanity. Heroic, tough, and unconquerable, Mithras attracted a great following among the army. His cult also stood for moral purity and chastity—a far cry from the sexual license that Brown claims pervaded Roman worship. Such cults did exist, but on the whole the Roman cults required adherence to moral standards.

It is no accident that some of the "mystery cults," such as that of Mithras, had many features in common with Christianity. Given this quest for hope and the desire to live according to a high moral code, the time was ripe for the spread of the Christian religion. Despite what Brown suggests, Constantine did not forcibly convert the pagan Romans. People were becoming Christian of their own will, for various reasons. People were increasingly experiencing spiritual unrest and were searching for something beyond the meaninglessness imposed by a yielding to impersonal fate. The Christian faith was appealing, and successful, because it was founded not on myths but on a historical person and datable events. It assured people of liberation from sin and redemption through the risen Jesus, and offered an ethical system that laid down clear, precise rules of conduct.

Although it had begun primarily as an urban phenomenon, Christianity eventually spread to the peasants in rural areas. It had also become socially acceptable as aristocratic resistance was overcome through the upward mobility of the middle classes who were Christian and were rising into the upper classes. Thus when Emperor Theodosius published his decree in 380 (see Q. 23), in a sense what he was doing was officially recognizing an existing reality: that the Christian faith had indeed triumphed over paganism on the grassroots level.

The major and obvious fact that *Da Vinci* conveniently ignores, of course, is the existence of Judaism, and it is from Judaism that Christianity developed, not from the attempt to suppress goddess religions. (See Part Eleven for questions about the Jewish tradition.)

28. How did pagan feasts and customs become Christian? Did this result from an imperial decree?

Let's take Easter first. No emperor ever passed legislation that deliberately "replaced" a pagan festival with Easter. From time immemorial, ancient peoples have celebrated important feasts at the time of the vernal equinox—the beginning of spring and of new life after the winter. At this time, pagan cultures celebrated the death and rising of a god. The Jewish people celebrated (and still celebrate) Passover each year on a date determined by the vernal equinox; this is the feast remembering when Yahweh gave them new life by rescuing them from slavery in Egypt. Because the passion, death, and resurrection of Jesus took place during the Passover feast, Christians have always celebrated Easter at this time—doubly appropriate because, as in pagan cultures, Easter commemorates the death and resurrection of God. The name "Easter" (German *Oster*) derives from the name of a North European fertility goddess whose festival had been held at this time to welcome spring and rebirth. In fact, out of respect for this established pre-Christian feast, the Christian missionaries to the Saxons adopted its name for their own festival.

The assignment of December 25 as the date for Christmas came about by papal, not imperial, decree. In the year 274 the Emperor Aurelian, realizing the benefits to the empire of promoting one important national cult, proclaimed December 25, the birthday of the Unconquered Sun, a national holiday. Here was another feast with significant connections to the natural year: this is the time of the winter solstice, the birthday of the sun, and the beginning of longer days, in which light—the sun—triumphed over the darkness of winter. When Pope Julius I (337–52) appointed a bishops' committee to set a date for celebrating Christ's birth, they decided to impart a Christian meaning to an established feast and so chose December 25. Far from selecting an arbitrary date or determining to "stamp out" paganism, the bishops in effect ratified what was already expressed in Christian theology and worship: that Christ was hailed as light-in-darkness, the Sun of Salvation and Sun of Righteousness, "visiting us like the dawn from on high" (see Luke 1:78).

Other pre-Christian festivals and customs were adapted to Christian belief by the people, especially the *pagani*—a word that originally meant "people of the countryside" (here Brown is correct)—who were accustomed to rural rituals associated with the natural year and particularly the agricultural cycle. It was natural for them to christianize what they had known as "pagan" (that is, rural) customs. A good example is the birthday of St. John the Baptist, celebrated at Midsummer, when the days are longest and about to wane. This pre-Christian festival, celebrated with bonfires, became christianized to commemorate the birth, six months before Jesus, of John who said of Jesus, "He must increase while I must decrease" (John 3:30)—just as the length of days is set to decrease after Midsummer.

29. Would Christians have regarded references to the sun as necessarily pagan and unchristian, as Brown indicates (p. 339)?

Throughout *The Da Vinci Code,* Dan Brown seems to be very unfamiliar with the ease with which Christians embraced and adapted pagan symbols and imagery for Christian purposes. In his very thorough and brilliant book on this topic, *Greek Myths and Christian Mystery,* Hugo Rahner emphasized the point that Christians *used* pagan myths to explain the truths of Christianity to their pagan neighbors. The sun was one of the premier symbols used by Christians to this end. Jesus Christ was the New Day, the Dawn from on High, the Light of the World. The Roman feast of the Unconquerable Sun was transformed into a feast honoring the birth of God on earth. Churches were built facing the east, whence would come the Savior.

30. So, were there no instances at all in which Christian beliefs were forced on pagan peoples?

Yes, there were. Instances of forced christianization have occurred in which pre-Christian beliefs were not respected. A notorious example is that of St. Boniface, missionary to the heathen Germans, who cut down their sacred tree and thus lost a marvelous opportunity to adapt it to the tree of Christ's crucifixion! But on the whole the Catholic Church has a good history of allowing its customs and traditions to grow and flourish from pre-Christian roots. One of the greatest prayer-gifts to the church has been the treasury of ancient Celtic customs and prayers, undeniably with pagan origins but encouraged and developed by Catholicism. Yet, as Celtic specialist Philip Newell points out in *The Book of Creation,* in nineteenth-century Scotland it was the rigid Calvinism that held sway there that attempted to suppress this tradition as pagan; these wonderful prayers have survived thanks to the diligent efforts of such transcribers as Alexander Carmichael.

So much of the richness of the Catholic tradition is owed to its capacity, as demonstrated over the centuries, to adapt for its own benefit elements of the preexisting cultures in which it has found itself. As one Jesuit theologian observed early in the twentieth century, it is because of this trait that Catholicism deservedly qualifies as a great world religion.

FIVE

THE "SACRED FEMININE"
AND WOMEN IN CHRISTIANITY

31. Dan Brown's characters accuse the church of eliminating the "sacred feminine" and the goddess from religion. How true is this?

Let's start with Teabing's statement (p. 238) that Christian philosophy decided to strip women of their honor as life-givers, an assertion that he explains by citing the Genesis account of creation in which Eve was fashioned from Adam's rib. In other words, Teabing qualifies his vague reference to "Christian philosophy" by giving an example from the Hebrew Scriptures, written several centuries before Christianity even existed! This muddled thinking is intensified by his implication that Genesis has made Adam into the creator in place of Eve.

The creation accounts in Genesis have nothing to do with presenting a false biology, as Teabing wants us to believe. These accounts are myths—that is, stories intended to present the timeless truth that *God* is the creator. Moreover, Genesis says that humans—of *both* sexes—were *made in the image of God*. The marvelous human mind has produced creation stories in many cultures in an attempt to explain how the world came to be. As heirs to the Jewish-Christian tradition we believe that the stories in our scriptures were actually inspired by God. What a pity that Dan Brown wants to reduce them to attempts to enforce an ideology! It was never a matter of eliminating goddesses but, rather, of a monotheistic tradition (belief in one God) prevailing over polytheistic traditions (belief in several gods). The people of Israel were special to their God because, unlike the polytheistic cultures that surrounded them, they adhered to belief in the one supreme God.

32. What positive feminine images are contained in the Old Testament?

The Hebrew Scriptures honor several great women as heroines in the history of Israel. Here are just a few of their stories:

The Book of Judith tells of the valiant widow Judith, who single-handedly saved the nation of Israel from destruction by the Assyrians. Holofernes, commander of the armies of King Nebuchadnezzar, set out on a punitive expedition against the nations that refused to participate in Assyria's war against the Medes. Meeting resistance from the Israelites, he laid siege to the town of Bethulia, where they were encamped. After thirty-four days, and with their water supply cut off, the Jews were ready to surrender. But at this point the beautiful, God-fearing Judith utterly opposed the notion that her people should give up rather than trust in the Lord. Dressing her hair and putting on her finest garments, she went to the Assyrian camp and offered to provide Holofernes with information that would lead him to final victory over the Jews. She advised him to bide his time.

After a few days Holofernes gave a banquet and invited Judith, intending to seduce her. But he landed in his bed in a drunken stupor, whereupon Judith beheaded him with his own sword. On learning what had happened, the Assyrians scattered in panic. They were overwhelmed by the Israelite army and their camp looted by the people. The high priest and Jewish elders praised Judith, through whom their God had granted them victory.

The Book of Esther tells of the courageous Jewish queen, consort of Persian King Xerxes (Ahasuerus) in the fifth century BC, who saved her people from destruction by a vengeful royal official. Two eunuchs at the royal court had been plotting against the king. When Mordecai, a Jewish servant of the king, discovered the plot, he informed the king, who had the eunuchs put to death. But Haman, the king's powerful vizier, sought revenge on Mordecai because of what had happened to the two eunuchs and because Mordecai refused to bow down and render to Haman the homage due to God alone. Thus Haman vowed to destroy all the

Jews in Xerxes' realm on a single day, and a lot, or *pur,* was cast to decide the day.

Queen Vashti, wife of King Xerxes, was deposed for refusing to obey an order of the king. From among many young women Esther was chosen to replace Vashti because of her beauty. Esther happened to be Mordecai's niece and adopted daughter. When word came to Esther from Mordecai about the plot to destroy the Jews, she put on mourning garments, covered her head with ashes, and prayed to the Lord God of Israel. She then donned her finery again, went to the king, and pleaded for the lives of her people. Esther had a sense that Divine Providence had granted her, a Jew, this position of royal favor precisely in order to intervene in this time of peril.

When Esther told the king about the plot and the reasons for it, he revoked Haman's decree against the Jews, had Haman put to death, and elevated Mordecai to Haman's position at the royal court. Queen Esther's courageous deed is commemorated on the feast of Purim, which means "lots."

The Second Book of Maccabees relates the fate of a heroic woman and her seven sons during the persecution of the Jews by the wicked king Antiochus Epiphanes. The seven brothers and their mother were arrested and tortured to force them to disregard God's law by eating pork. Instead, each brother in turn eloquently voiced his disdain for the king's orders and his fidelity to the God of Israel. The mother watched each of her seven sons perish that day while she urged them to be true to their God, who would give them everlasting life. Finally the mother, too, was put to death. The scriptural author is full of praise for the courageous mother, whom he calls "admirable and worthy of honorable memory" (2 Macc 7:20). This amazing story of martyrdom became an inspiration to the early Christians, who often risked a similar gruesome fate.

33. What memorable images of women does the New Testament offer us?

Obviously we have Mary the mother of Jesus and Mary Magdalene, both of whom will be discussed separately (see QQ. 36, 37, 39, 40, and Part Six)! The New Testament—especially the Acts of the Apostles and some references in St. Paul's letters—also shows other women assuming significant leadership roles among the first Christians.

One of these was Prisca (or Priscilla). She and her husband, Aquila, had been living in Rome, but when the emperor Claudius expelled all the Jews from the city, they left and settled in Corinth. They were leaders of a house-church, and, since house-churches were then the basic units of organization among the Christians, Prisca and Aquila would have been prominent members of the local Christian community. In fact, Paul contacted them upon his arrival in Corinth. Since he and Aquila were both tentmakers, Paul stayed with them and worked with Aquila at their common trade. Prisca and Aquila accompanied Paul when he left Corinth for Ephesus. There they met an Alexandrian Jew named Apollos. An eloquent speaker and knowledgeable about the scriptures, Apollos preached the good news but only knew the baptism of John. It was Prisca and Aquila who taught him more fully about the new Way of Jesus, and they must have been very effective, because Paul's First Letter to the Corinthians suggests that Apollos became a charismatic teacher in the church there. In his Letter to the Romans Paul refers to Prisca and Aquila as his coworkers in Jesus and says that they risked their necks for his life.

The Acts of the Apostles relates how, when Paul and his company landed at the Roman colony of Philippi, they went down to the river and met a group of women who had gathered there. One of these was Lydia, a "God-fearing" woman from Thyatira and thus a Gentile living on the edges of Jewish society. Upon listening openly and eagerly to Paul's preaching, she was converted to the new Way and was baptized along with her household. Lydia's home town, located in modern-day Turkey, was a prosperous center of trade and craft guilds in Asia Minor. She herself was a business-woman who dealt in purple cloth, and thus she was financially independent and head of her own household; in other words, she was a woman well positioned to assume a key role among the early Christians. After her baptism she prevailed upon Paul and his companions to stay at her house. Later, after his release from the prison where he had been thrown for allegedly creating a disturbance, it was to Lydia's house that Paul repaired. In the Book of Revelation Thyatira is the location of one of the seven churches that Jesus addresses, praising their faith, love, and service. It's interesting to speculate whether Lydia may have eventually returned to her home town and helped establish Christianity there.

Finally, at the close of his Letter to the Romans Paul mentions Phoebe, "our sister," who was a deacon or minister of the church at Cenchreae. Cenchreae was one of the two port cities for Corinth, so that it may well have been a key center for early Christianity in which Phoebe acted in a leadership capacity. Paul describes her with a word that means "patroness," and scholars speculate: Did she contribute money for missionary purposes? Lend hospitality? Intervene with the secular authorities? At any rate, Paul enjoins the Christians at Rome to help her in any way she needs; he may have written the Letter to the Romans from Corinth or Cenchreae, and Phoebe may well have been the bearer of the letter to Rome.

With these and other women among his trusted and treasured colleagues in the Lord, it's no wonder that Paul could write to the Galatians, "There is neither Jew nor Greek…neither slave nor free…*neither male nor female*…all are one in Christ Jesus" (Gal 3:28).

The biblical stories about heroic women and women in positions of respect demonstrate clearly that revering the feminine isn't about worshipping goddesses or about sex with sacred prostitutes. When we consider the tradition of venerating Mary and the women saints, these biblical women, and the many prominent women in church history, show how impoverished Dan Brown's one-sided, woman-as-sex-object notion of the "sacred feminine" turns out to be.

34. Can you talk about some of these prominent women in church history?

Most people don't realize what high positions of authority women were allowed to occupy in the Middle Ages when the monastery rather than the cathedral usually occupied the center of Christian life. A number of abbesses played very influential roles in the history of the church.

One of these was Hilda, abbess of Whitby (614–80) in the north of England. Whitby was a "double monastery," an institution of both monks and nuns. This style of monastic life had been imported from Gaul (France), where these monasteries had usually been founded by high-born women and were thus ruled by abbesses. All double monasteries in England were headed by abbesses.

A great-niece of the king of Northumbria, Hilda had been a married woman before becoming a nun at age thirty-three. By the time she became abbess of Whitby, she was known throughout Britain for her extraordinary knowledge as well as her charity. Under Hilda's leadership Whitby became an important center of learning, producing at least five bishops and numerous theologians and other scholars. She had a huge library built there and encouraged a cowherd on the farm to develop his poetic gifts; he was Caedmon, the first English poet. During Hilda's tenure, the famous Synod of Whitby was held in 664. Attended by royalty as well as by leading churchmen, this synod decided many pressing issues, including ensuring that the church in England followed the Roman system in the dating of Easter.

By the time of Hildegard of Bingen (1098–1179), the age when abbesses exerted great power in the church and society was over. Yet, the twelfth century saw the career of this amazingly influential Benedictine nun, who wryly described herself as a "poor, shy woman" who nonetheless preached to the most prominent men of her day. Born in the Rhineland, Hildegard took religious vows in her late teens and, in 1136, was elected superior of the convent near Bingen. In 1141 she received her prophetic call to write down the visions she had been receiving from God since her youth, and began dictating the visions to her secretary in what was to be her most famous book, *Scivias*. When she consulted Bernard of Clairvaux, the leading spiritual authority of the era, about her visions, Bernard recognized them as authentic and commended her to Pope Eugenius III, who endorsed Hildegard's work and authorized her to continue it.

At a time when women did not play any public role in ecclesiastical affairs, Hildegard preached in the public squares and in cathedrals and churches. The only woman at this time to do full preaching tours with ecclesiastical approval, she also wrote letters of counsel to people from all walks of life. Neither pope nor emperor was exempt from her stern rebukes when the situation required it. God had chosen Hildegard because the times desperately needed a prophet to preach reform. Intense strife raged between the emperor and the popes, and bitter strife within the church as well. Blaming clerical corruption for the rise of heresy among laypeople, Hildegard pictured the church as a beautiful but battered woman, her torn clothes symbolizing clerical abuse.

Taking her imagery from the beautiful green Rhineland in which she lived, Hildegard also wrote much about the interconnectedness of all things and human responsibility for the care of creation; thus she can be considered the forerunner of today's ecotheologians.

35. Did any laywomen enjoy influential positions in the church?

The feast of Corpus Christi and the beautiful hymns written for it by St. Thomas Aquinas are immensely popular in Catholic liturgical devotion, but what isn't as well known is that the feast owes its establishment to a group of women. In the late twelfth century laypeople, especially women, were increasingly seeking new forms of piety and new ways of being religious. One very popular movement for laywomen was the Beguines, who began at this time in the flourishing city of Liège in Belgium. The Beguines sought to live under some religious discipline, and to practice poverty, chastity, and a penitential life of prayer. One of them was Juliana of Cornillon (ca. 1193–1258), a holy woman who served at a leper hospital. Several times Juliana had a eucharistic vision of the moon in all its splendor but with a small segment darkened. Christ revealed to her that the moon represented the church, and the darkened segment a missing feast that he wished to have celebrated. Such visions, particularly among laywomen, were not uncommon in the High Middle Ages. Juliana and her followers had been pressing for the establishment of a eucharistic feast, and they interpreted her vision as a sign that Christ himself supported their efforts. With the help and support of the bishop of Liège, the local Dominicans, and an archdeacon who became Pope Urban IV, the feast of Corpus Christi was elevated to one of universal observance.

We sometimes think of mystics as living an ivory-tower existence isolated in prayer and ecstasy, but for many medieval mystics nothing could be further from the truth. Catherine of Siena (1347–80) was an activist who cared for the sick and the poor. Siena had been hit especially hard in the Black Death of 1347; Catherine looked after plague victims and those suffering from other diseases. She was a laywoman—a Third Order Dominican—whom God called to preach to all people, but especially to the hierarchy. Pope and bishops alike needed to contribute to church reform, to watch diligently for clerical misconduct in order to stop it.

One irregularity that Catherine sought to remedy was that the popes were living in France and not in Rome. In 1308 Pope Clement V transferred the papal court to Avignon, initially as a temporary residence while he solved the problems raised by France's powerful King Philip. But once the popes were established in

Avignon, various factors tended to keep them there, including turbulence in Italy and intrigue in France. This became known as the Babylonian Captivity, a period when the church lost its international prestige and its moral authority. Convinced that as long as the papacy remained in France it would be too influenced by political concerns to be in a position to implement necessary reforms, Catherine played a major role in urging Pope Gregory XI (1370–77) to return to Rome. In so doing, she single-handedly changed the course of history.

Hilda, Hildegard, Juliana, Catherine, and countless others witness to one important fact: The Catholic Church did offer women a variety of opportunities to participate and make their influence felt, sometimes on a large scale. It was the Protestant Reformation that relegated women solely to the domestic sphere and deprived them of these kinds of opportunities.

36. With all the talk in the novel about "the sacred feminine," isn't it odd that Mary the mother of Jesus isn't mentioned?

Actually, it's not odd at all when you consider that mention of Mary would give the lie to Brown's claims! Margaret Starbird, one of Teabing's "historical sources," refers to the Virgin Mary as "the only Goddess image allowed in Christianity" (*Woman with the Alabaster Jar,* p. xxii). Ironically, this is one tidbit of "goddess information" Brown didn't pick up on, undoubtedly less because it's a tidbit of *mis*information (Mary has never been worshipped as a goddess) than because Mary's exalted role in Christianity would have been a most inconvenient reality for him to have to deal with. Brown claims that the church in the fourth century moved to minimize Christ's humanity and make him divine. The truth is that the church, from early days, stressed Jesus' birth through Mary, a human mother, precisely in order to defend his humanity against the heresy of Docetism, which held that Jesus only *appeared to be* human. The Niceno-Constantinopolitan

Creed, formulated in 381, states that Jesus became "incarnate of the Holy Spirit and the Virgin Mary, and was made man."

Let's be clear: God's plan for redeeming the human race could not have been realized without the young girl from Nazareth's *fiat* ("yes") to the question: Will you become the mother of the Redeemer? For this reason the church throughout the ages has exalted Mary. This fact couldn't possibly have found a place in Dan Brown's accusations about the church and the "sacred feminine."

37. Sometimes devotion to Mary seems to lose sight of connection with Jesus. What about the Rosary? Does this devotion affirm Mary's connection with the incarnation and redemption?

Indeed it does, although, as with anything human, the Rosary, too, is open to misuse and misinterpretation. There are, for example, well-meaning pious people who believe that Mary "gave us" the Rosary, as if it were a ready-made, revealed-from-heaven product. In fact, the evolution of the Rosary has a rich history. In the early church the Psalms were *the* prayer book for Christians. The Rosary went through many versions, developing as substitutes for the 150 Psalms — 150 Hail Marys, with the Our Father before and Glory Be after each decade in order to ensure that it retained its christological character. Eventually the mysteries were added, again in various stages until its final development into the Joyful, Sorrowful, and Glorious Mysteries. Yet, even this wasn't final, since in October 2002 Pope John Paul II added the new Luminous Mysteries to highlight important events in Christ's public ministry, stating that the Rosary exists "to proclaim, and even cry out, before the world that Jesus Christ is Lord and Saviour, 'the way, and the truth and the life' (John 14:6)" (Apostolic Letter *Rosarium Virginis Mariae* §1).

The church has always been concerned to ensure that the Rosary is christologically based and consonant with scripture. All of the mysteries are rooted in scripture except for the fourth and fifth Glorious Mysteries (Mary's assumption into heaven and her crowning as Queen of Heaven), and even these are rooted in ancient Christian traditions.

Some fascinating insights about Mary's assumption have come from an unexpected source—the Swiss psychologist Carl Jung (1875–1961). He was overjoyed when the church defined this dogma in 1950. Apparently he considered it the most important event in the western world since the Reformation. Jung maintained that the assumption of Mary's physical body into heaven signified the *hieros gamos*—the union of the heavenly bride with the bridegroom—and that this represents, on a psychic archetypal level, the inclusion of a feminine element into the masculine Godhead. Unlike Brown's reference to the *hieros gamos* in terms of a sex ritual, Jung was hailing the potential for humanity to integrate the masculine and feminine in the human psyche in such a way that wars and other patriarchal methods of resolving conflicts would be discarded in favor of more peaceful and balanced ways. Jung believed that the elevation of Mary's assumption to official Catholic dogma signified the beginning of such an era in human history.

38. The novel contains a flashback in which Langdon is teaching a class and discussing religions that revere the earth. He mentions May Day and the celebration of new life in spring (pp. 95–96). Surely Christianity is aware of nature as a revelation of God?

Of course. Christians celebrate the central mystery of their faith—the dying and rising of Jesus—in the spring, just as the earth is starting to burgeon with new life. This is no coincidence! As the earth after its winter rest now bursts with life, so does Jesus, who has died for our sins, rise again. Jesus is the fruit that the earth has yielded (Ps 67).

Catholics speak of the "sacramentality" of creation. A sacrament is a visible sign of an invisible reality (God). We regard created things—visible reality—as revealing to us aspects of the invisible God: for example, a meadow in bloom reveals God's beauty; the sea shows us God's power; the mountains speak to us of God's majesty. This capacity of created things to reveal God is the foundation for our Catholic "ecotheology" that enjoins us to care for the environment. This is no invention of tree huggers— you can trace it as far back as St. Thomas Aquinas and beyond, to the early church fathers!

39. To return to the question of Mary: Brown seems to suggest that, because Christianity doesn't worship goddesses, it doesn't revere nature. How does the mother of Jesus fit into our reverence for creation?

Because Brown chooses to overlook completely the existence of Mary, he misses out on the rich tradition associating her with the natural world. Most importantly in this context, Catholics celebrate May as Mary's month precisely because of her femininity and its association with nature's fertility and productivity. May is a month unparalleled for awareness of nature; the earth is then at its peak of returning to life after winter's sleep. Pre-Christian Europeans celebrated a spring fertility festival on May Day, and in some rural places Maypoles are still a tradition. That Christians should come to associate this month with Mary was inevitable.

Nineteenth-century converts, so anxious to emphasize Mary's connection with the mystery of her Son, were concerned about explaining this celebration of Mary in May. After all, there is no liturgical basis for it. The important christological feasts of Mary—the annunciation, the purification, for example—don't fall in May. And so they offered explanations based on the abundance of life in nature during this month. John Henry Newman pointed out that May is an extraordinarily beautiful month, and "such gladness and joyousness of external Nature is a fit attendant on our devotion" to Mary ("Meditations on the Litany of Loreto"). In his poem "The May Magnificat" the Jesuit poet Gerard Manley Hopkins observed that nature during May is in its high-powered reproductive mode, and thus the world in May recalls Mary pregnant with Christ and reminds her of it. Nature's motherhood is a sacrament of Mary's motherhood! Moreover, in his other great Marian poem "The Blessed Virgin Compared to the Air We Breathe," Hopkins declares that Mary's presence and power are greater than that of any goddess was ever reckoned to be.

Ancient tradition has conferred on Mary titles associated with the natural world. One of the most famous is "Mystical Rose," the rose without thorns that symbolizes human innocence before Adam and Eve's fall. Hopkins wrote an early poem, "Rosa Mystica," in which he follows an old Anglo-Saxon tradition that identifies Christ as the blossom and Mary as the tree that gave it birth. The ancient Christian tradition of Mary as Mystical Rose and its association with nature is far richer and infinitely more real than Brown's contrived information byte that *Rose* is an anagram of *Eros* (p. 254); since this doesn't hold true for the majority of languages, how can it have any universal significance?

Let's end this discussion with a reference to an old and very popular Marian hymn, "Bring Flowers of the Rarest." Many of us remember this from May crownings of days gone by: "O Mary, we crown thee with blossoms today, Queen of the Angels, Queen of the May." The Irish singer Phil Coulter—who includes an instrumental of this hymn on one of his albums—testifies to its continuing popularity, and at his concerts it's one song with which many in the audience are guaranteed to sing along. Unlike the sugary Victorian "mother" images no longer relevant in an age when women balance the challenges of motherhood with those of professional careers, the association of Mary with nature and the identification of her with the archetypal Queen of Nature/Mother Earth are timeless.

40. Does Catholic devotion to Mary have only positive aspects?

It's just as well to acknowledge that Marian devotion has had its downsides. The image of virgin *and* mother, while certainly a reason to revere Mary, has perhaps unwittingly made Catholic women feel inadequate in having held up for them a model that, in this respect anyway, can't possibly be imitated (see Q. 58). Another unfortunate Marian model held up for women in the nineteenth century was the Victorian domestic ideal of women as passive and submissive. In our own time, Mary's image has been in danger of being sullied by so-called visionaries who see her as a punishing mother, threatening dire consequences if certain injunctions are not obeyed.

But we can be thankful for our positive contemporary images of Mary that nourish our spirituality and can serve as inspirational role models: the feisty Jewish woman of Nazareth, mother of a sometimes perplexing Son, woman of liberation whose *Magnificat* canticle celebrates a God who turns the existing order in the world upside down.

41. Langdon claims that the church has demonized the "sacred feminine" because woman's ability to produce life posed a threat to the male church (p. 238). How does this accusation square with the Catholic Church's stand on related women's issues?

The Catholic Church has always staunchly supported the integrity of the family, and its teaching on related issues has been aimed at women's welfare and that of the children they bear. The church objects to divorce in order to protect women and children, to ensure that they do not become discarded and economically impoverished. By its strong stand against abortion the church wants to protect women against two evils in particular: (1) from being reduced to and treated as sex objects—or, as one postabortive woman graphically and poignantly expressed it, being treated as something to be vacuumed out and reused, like a rented car; and (2) from suffering the post-traumatic stress disorder that all too often follows in the wake of an abortion and is then known as postabortion syndrome. The church's objection to abortion also protects the developing fetus—the life that a woman is bearing and nurturing—from being treated as a disposable object. Church teaching in this context can hardly be considered as demeaning to women as life-givers.

42. Surely the church's attitude toward women can't always have been unfailingly positive?

Indeed, feminist and other scholars have justification for many of their critiques of the historical church. Some theologians in the early centuries exalted celibacy in such a way as to imply that women must be avoided because they are the temptress who will lead the man astray. St. Jerome was responsible for the formulation of the doctrine of Mary's perpetual virginity, and the strong likelihood must be admitted that St. Augustine, arguably the greatest mind produced by the Western church, was working out his own conflicts about sex in his writings.

If elements in early Christianity held celibacy to be an ideal state superior to marriage, this was not unique to the church, despite what Dan Brown would have us believe: the church was reflecting the patriarchal thought that pervaded the era. But how, then, would Brown explain the strong appeal that early Christianity had for women? Robin Lane Fox in *Pagans and Christians* notes that in the third century, women made up a "clear majority" in the churches. One of many possible explanations of this is the fact that Jesus himself was woman-friendly. He was loving, compassionate, and forgiving; contemporary psychologists would say that Jesus was someone whose masculine and feminine aspects were perfectly integrated. He presented a striking contrast to the pagan warrior gods, many of whom are also depicted as rapists.

True, the church in more recent times has no longer been the same place as that which respected such powerful, influential women as Hilda and Hildegard (see Q. 37). If we read the history of women's religious orders and the attempts of these feisty women to establish their presence and their ministries in nine-teenth-century America, for example, we see that for as many as received support from the local hierarchy, there were as many, or more, that found institutional opposition one of the numerous obstacles against which they had to struggle. And yet, ultimately they succeeded, and it can safely be argued that the presence of so many educated women not only in the church but in American society today is one of the enduring legacies of these pioneer educators. This, in the end, is what's important—not some red-herring argument about the church and the "sacred feminine."

43. Many women today are angry with the church. Why is this so?

There are a number of issues about which women believe, with some justification, that the church has treated them unfairly. On the abortion question, for example, some view the church as coming across as more concerned with the developing fetus than with the mother and, perhaps, with the welfare of the children she already has, even in a life-vs.-death situation.

Many women regard the church's attempt to suppress any discussion of woman's ordination—as deacons as well as priests—as less than theologically honest; the limitation of official preaching faculties to ordained men is unquestionably depriving Catholics in the pews of some extraordinarily gifted and sensitive voices.

Another controversial issue concerns the status of lay church employees (here "lay" includes religious sisters, who are nonor-dained), who are all too frequently subject to the injustices of low salaries and unjust working conditions (meaning, among other things, virtually no employment security). The overwhelming majority of these lay employees are women, and it must be recognized that the church's prophetic teachings on social justice tend to fall short of being applied to its own employees. This particular matter is, of course, an issue within the local church—the diocese or parish—and cannot be laid at the door of "church doctrine."

As these examples show, if one wants to level against the church the accusation that it "demeans women," then one must speak in terms of its impact on *real, human women* and not on some ethereal level of an imaginary smear campaign against an amorphous concept of the "sacred feminine." All the goddess worship in the world is meaningless if it doesn't translate into proper respect for and treatment of real women. The early church, following Jesus' example and the writings and deeds of St. Paul, did much to elevate the treatment of women over what it had been in the pagan world.

44. Brown accuses the church of perpetrating a great bloodbath against women in the form of the witch hunts (p. 125). What was the book *Malleus Maleficarum* that apparently brought this about?

First, let's look at the historical background. What we now call "witchcraft" had several different meanings in the early centuries of the Christian era. It may often have meant little more than use of charms, spells, or herbs to bring about good or evil effects. While secular rulers including such Frankish rulers as Charlemagne enacted severe laws against witchcraft practices, the church's attitude was relatively lenient and moderate. Sometimes the church regarded these folk beliefs and practices as superstitious relics of paganism and tried to wean the people away from them; at other times it viewed witchcraft as an evil that needed to be suppressed. To a great extent, it depended on how one defined "witchcraft."

A transformation in the church's attitude toward witchcraft occurred between the twelfth and the fifteenth centuries. In the twelfth century, contact with Arabic culture generated interest in "natural magic" like alchemy and astrology—that is, in phenomena that could no longer be tolerated as mere peasant superstition. The rise of the dualist heresy, which held that the devil was an equal opponent to God, meant that witches were now regarded as having made a pact with the Evil One and had thereby renounced God. Witches thus became associated not merely with evil in general but with Satan himself, the Prince of Evil.

This "either/or" view—one is loyal *either* to the good God *or* to God's equal opponent, Satan—led to witches being accused of heresy. Thus the charge of heresy was primary, and the *maleficium,* or the practice of evil whereby witches harmed people, was secondary, a by-product.

Once the accusation of heresy was involved, witchcraft became subject to the Inquisition, and thus the church's official policy was changed. In 1484 two Dominican friars, Heinrich Kraemer and Jakob Sprenger, persuaded Pope Innocent VIII to issue a bull deploring the spread of witchcraft in Germany and authorizing them to root it out. In 1486 Kraemer and Sprenger published *Malleus Maleficarum,* a detailed legal and theological document and compendium of the folklore and beliefs of the Alpine peasants. Inspired by Exodus 22:18 as its motto—"You shall not permit a female sorcerer to live"—the *Malleus* was regarded as the standard, authoritative handbook on witchcraft until well into the eighteenth century. It did much to spur on witch-hunting hysteria in Europe, even though its original intention was to deal primarily with heresy.

Malleus Maleficarum recognized that men as well as women could be witches who derived their powers from associating, and especially through sexual relationships, with the devil. Although initiated by Catholics, the campaign against witches was by no means limited to the church but was adopted and extended by Protestants, who carried it into the New World where it culminated in the notorious New England witch trials.

Malleus Maleficarum was certainly not the most pleasant of documents produced in the history of the church, and, admittedly, its effects far surpassed what its authors ever intended. But Brown's account of it is grossly inaccurate and exaggerated and, indeed, in a few short paragraphs he himself seems caught up in the same kind of hysteria that the work generated in the medieval and early modern periods.

No one has any precise idea of the number of people burnt as witches, but the latest conclusion of scholarly research is 40,000. Brown's figure of five million women is a great exaggeration, as is his charge that *Malleus Maleficarum* is the most blood-soaked publication in history (p. 125; has he never heard of Hitler's *Mein Kampf?*). Least credible of all are his lists of the types of people adversely affected by *Malleus Maleficarum*. This publication did not put an end to a female Catholic priesthood, and since neither Orthodox rabbis nor Islamic clerics of either sex would have come under the church's authority, the claim of an attempt by the church to abolish female rabbis and Islamic clerics (who, at any rate, did not exist) is nonsense. Moreover, this was the age in which mysticism flourished in the church—and the mystics included such great female saints as Julian of Norwich, Catherine of Siena, and Catherine of Genoa—so that inclusion of "mystics" among those whom the church considered witches is wide of the mark, to say the least.

SIX

MARY MAGDALENE

45. Could Jesus have been married to Mary Magdalene? Leigh Teabing asserts that their marriage is "part of the historical record" (p. 245). Jewish custom at the time, he claims, forbade a man to remain unmarried.

Nowhere is a marriage between Jesus and Mary Magdalene mentioned in any historical records. Not even the legends about Mary Magdalene from southern France, which Brown touts as the epitome of recorded memories of her, contain any indication that she had been Jesus' wife. Only in the twentieth century did the idea of a romantic relationship or even marriage begin to be overtly expressed, with such popular works as the novel *The Last Temptation of Christ* (Kazantzákis, 1951) or the rock opera *Jesus Christ Superstar* (Webber and Rice, 1971), both of which were later made into films.

Like the conflation, or combining, of three biblical women into one that produced the popular "composite" image of Mary Magdalene (see QQ. 54, 55, 58), the construction of close familial relationships among important persons is not an uncommon phenomenon; for example, medieval sagas and epics may present, as brothers, kings who lived several generations apart, thereby collapsing time. Even in the Hebrew Scriptures we find three undeniably historical figures—Abraham, Isaac, and Jacob—spoken of as occupying three consecutive generations: grandfather, father, and son. This may be true, or more likely it may be the biblical writer's way of demonstrating a close relationship among prominent persons in Israel's history who in fact lived many generations apart. It seems to be the human mind's way of formulating a "shorthand" in an effort to understand more easily the significance of certain persons and events.

46. But would Jesus have been disobeying an important Jewish custom by remaining unmarried?

It's true that marriage would have been the norm for a first-century Jew, but that doesn't mean that an unmarried male Jew would have been regarded as abnormal or scandalous. There are several valid reasons why Jesus could have remained unmarried.

Jesus was an itinerant preacher who regarded himself as entrusted by God with a special revelation about the inbreaking of God's kingdom: "The kingdom of God is at hand," the world is about to undergo a fundamental transformation. The Gospels indicate that Jesus believed this event to be imminent: the old world would pass away, would be transformed into something new, and it would happen very soon, possibly even within the lifetime of the present generation. Because of this inbreaking of the new order, and his special role in preaching it, Jesus could well have deemed it wise to abstain from a relationship such as marriage.

There was, in fact, a Jewish sect called the Essenes whose lifestyle reflected an eschatological attitude—that is, they expected the imminent arrival of the new order. The Essenes at Qumran—the site associated with the Dead Sea Scrolls, as these Essene documents are known—were, for the most part, celibate males leading a communal life. Some scripture scholars suggest that Jesus may have been influenced by the Essenes, as his cousin John the Baptist almost certainly was.

Who could have been a more exemplary Jew than St. Paul? Yet, he never married. In his First Letter to the Corinthians he indicates that it is better not to marry, and he offers similar reasons to those above: the second coming of Jesus was expected to occur within the present generation; thus the world as people knew it would pass away, and it was preferable not to complicate one's life with marriage.

Given the eschatological mind-set at the time, and the self-perceived role of preachers and teachers like Jesus and Paul, it was not at all unthinkable or "unnatural" for some Jewish men to choose not to marry, and this has *nothing whatever* to do with any notion of the celibate state being inherently superior to, or more virtuous than, marriage.

47. Might there have been, as Brown claims, a royal dynasty descended from Jesus and Mary Magdalene? According to Brown, the church suppressed this information because the existence of a child of Jesus would have endangered the church's promotion of Jesus as divine (p. 254).

Basing his story on the spurious assertions in *Holy Blood, Holy Grail,* Brown claims that Mary Magdalene, pregnant with Jesus' child, traveled to southern France and there gave birth to a daughter. The Jews in France, he says, revered Mary as royalty and as the mother of a royal dynasty (p. 255). In the fifth century this dynasty supposedly intermarried with French royals and created the Merovingian dynasty (p. 257).

Assuming that there really were any Jews in present-day France in the first century—which is doubtful—let's stop and consider how they would have reacted to the presence of Mary Magdalene and her child. Jesus, Mary's alleged husband, had been horribly executed as a common criminal. Rejected by the leaders of his own people, he had died believing his mission to have failed. If this were the case in Palestine, why would any Jews as far away as France have regarded his "wife" as royalty?

48. But what of the royal dynasty mentioned by Brown? Who were the Merovingians?

The notion of "French royal blood" in the fifth century is anachronistic, to say the least. For one thing, the Merovingians, called after a semimythical ancestor named Merovech and dating from the middle of the fifth century, were only one of several dynasties among the many tribes of Franks. The Franks were one of many *Germanic* nations who settled along the Rhine River and gradually occupied what is now Belgium as well as parts of France. The Merovingian king Clovis was only one of several rival Frankish kings when he succeeded his father as king over this group of Franks in about 481, but gradually, by military means, he extended his rule by overthrowing the local rulers. Clovis was responsible for his people's conversion to Christianity.

Unlike the other Germanic barbarian tribes, the Franks were the first barbarians to convert directly from paganism to Catholic Christianity rather than to Arianism (see Q. 26). This placed them in favor with the Roman population of the territories they had taken over and, even more importantly, with the ecclesiastical and civic authorities. Thus the process was set in motion by which church and state eventually formed a union out of which Christendom emerged.

By the middle of the sixth century the Merovingians were the most powerful of the barbarian kings. But despite these early strong rulers, over the centuries the Merovingian dynasty gradually weakened—probably through intermarriage—until the kings were mere puppets and the real power was in the hands of the chief administrator of the royal household. One of these was Charles Martel, who repelled the Muslim advance into Europe in 732. After his death, Charles's two sons set up a puppet Merovingian king and took over the real power. In 747 one of them abdicated, leaving his brother Pepin as sole ruler. This marked the formal beginning of the Carolingian dynasty. Pepin deposed the last of the powerless Merovingian kings and had himself elected king of the Franks in 751. His grandson, Charlemagne, was crowned head of the Holy Roman Empire in 800.

The sixth-century historian Gregory of Tours chronicled the complicated saga of the Merovingian kings and their people in his *History of the Franks,* and Gregory provides no hint whatever that these tall blond rulers (the kings never cut their hair and were thus known as the "long-haired kings") ever intermarried with an olive-skinned dynasty of Semitic people. Surely the presence of such unusual, even exotic people in the region would not have escaped the attention of this exhaustively thorough chronicler.

49. And why is there such a strong connection between Mary Magdalene and France? Is it true that the Catholic Church tried to suppress this information?

Many countries have claimed visits by important early friends of Christ. Spaniards have long maintained that St. James the Greater preached in Spain or that his remains were buried in Compostela; the English claim that Joseph of Arimathea came to Glastonbury; Christians in India trace their religious ancestry back to St. Thomas the Apostle; and the French claim that Mary Magdalene visited Provence. Scholars since the seventeenth century have seriously doubted the French claim, but what is interesting for the purposes of Brown's novel is that the Catholic Church rigorously defended the claim, even to the point of suspending the teaching faculties of the famous nineteenth-century Catholic historian Père Duchesne for two years because he claimed that there was no evidence to support the presence of Mary Magdalene in France. Thus, rather than suppressing the legend of a visit by Mary Magdalene to France, the Church actively supported it well beyond reasonable limits.

50. Did Jesus entrust to Mary Magdalene the task of founding the church, as Brown asserts (p. 254)?

It was Jesus himself who preached the kingdom of God. Christianity evolved when Jesus' followers, after his death, preserved his teachings and preached the good news of our salvation through Jesus' victory on the cross. Brown's language, claiming that Jesus intended that someone "found" a church and that he left it in a particular person's "hands," suggests that he was setting up a corporation and appointing persons to certain executive positions—hardly the way to speak about someone who came to preach the good news of our salvation, free us from the futility of our sin and death, and gather his followers together as the people of God.

The task that Jesus entrusted to Mary Magdalene was that of telling his other disciples that he had risen from the dead. In Matthew's Gospel, she and "the other Mary" (the mother of James and Joseph, 27:56) receive this charge first from an angel at the tomb (28:7) and then from Jesus himself (28:19). Mark's Gospel gives two versions: in one, the angel tells Mary Magdalene and two other women that they are to announce to Jesus' "disciples and Peter" that he will meet them in Galilee (16:7); in the longer ending of Mark, Jesus appears first to Mary Magdalene, after which she tells the news to his followers (16:9–10). Luke recounts how the women, of whom he singles out Mary Magdalene and two others, were told by the angel at the tomb that Jesus had risen; after this the women convey the news to the apostles (24:5, 10).

Note how in all these accounts Mary Magdalene's name appears first—evidence of her preeminent position among these early women followers of Jesus. But it is in the Gospel of John that the risen Jesus appears to Mary Magdalene alone and tells her, "Go to my brothers and say to them, 'I am ascending to my Father and your Father, to my God and your God'" (20:17).

51. Brown and his characters are forever using such phrases as "the historical record" in connection with his assertion. Do we, on our part, have any proof that these gospel accounts are true?

In judging the historicity of an event mentioned in the Gospels—that is, in determining whether it is likely actually to have happened—scripture scholars have two rules: (1) The more frequently an event is mentioned, the more likely it is to be true. (2) The more unusual the event is in terms of the norms of the time, the more likely it is to be true. The charge to the women to spread the news of Jesus' resurrection is preserved in *all four Gospels*. And the fact that this responsibility is *given to women* is most unusual indeed: Jewish law of that time did not accept women's testimony as valid.

Thus the recurrence of this event in all four Gospels, and the unusual circumstances associated with it, testify to its historicity. No one who had wanted to make up a story about Jesus rising from the dead would have put this message in the mouths of women. So here we have, *contra* Brown and his assertions, the strongest possible support for the claim of the Christian tradition about Mary Magdalene's true significance in the early Christian community.

52. Might Mary of Magdala have occupied a position of leadership in the early church?

Very much so! As we have seen through St. Paul's writings (see Q. 33), women did play important roles in the early church, and there is every reason to believe that Mary Magdalene was one of them, as Mary R. Thompson deftly contends in her book *Mary of Magdala: What* The Da Vinci Code *Misses.* Thompson cites various pieces of evidence that suggest Mary Magdalene's prominent role in the first Christian community.

It was the priest-theologian Hippolytus of Rome (ca. 170–ca. 235) who first hailed Mary Magdalene as "apostle to the apostles," because of Jesus' charge to her to announce the good news of his resurrection to his other disciples (see Q. 50). Thompson points out that Mary indeed qualifies for the name of "apostle" in the sense in which St. Paul uses the term in his letters. For Paul, to be an apostle one must have "seen the Lord." In his First Letter to the Corinthians, Paul asks, "Am I not an apostle? Have I not seen Jesus our Lord?" (9:1). It is on this that he bases his own claim to apostleship: he has seen the Lord. An apostle is one chosen to proclaim something that he or she has actually witnessed, and after Jesus appeared to her and entrusted her with the good news of his resurrection, Mary Magdalene went and "announced to the disciples, 'I have seen the Lord'" (John 20:18).

Thompson notes that in John's Gospel it was women who made important statements about who Jesus was. The woman at the well told her fellow Samaritans, "Come and see a man who told me everything I have ever done! He cannot be the Messiah, can he?" (John 4:29). Martha confesses her belief in Jesus as "the Messiah, the Son of God, the one coming into the world" (John 11:27). And Mary Magdalene solemnly announces that Jesus has risen: "I have seen the Lord" (John 20:18). Mary's position as chief witness to this crucial fact of the risen Lord secured her place of significance in the early Christian community, a significance that could not be and was not ignored by the authors of the Gospels.

The fact that the Gospels consistently refer to Mary Magdalene as "Mary of Magdala" is evidence of her importance in the early church (cf. Matt 27:56, 61; 28:1; Mark 15:40, 47; 16:1; Luke 8:2; 24:10; John 19:25; 20:1, 18). This appellation indicates that most members of the communities for which the Gospels were written would have recognized who she was—a disciple who had had a leadership role in the earliest church. "Mary of Magdala"—her first name plus the place from which she came—had achieved the status of being identified by a technical term just as in our own time "Mother Theresa of Calcutta" is instantly recognizable as the nun who served the destitute dying and played a prophetic role in the church of the late twentieth century.

As theologian Elizabeth Johnson points out in terms of the biblical accounts of the resurrection, it is Mary Magdalene and Jesus' other women disciples who keep the story going after Jesus' death. Led by Mary Magdalene, the women are essential to the continuity of the narrative, because, having looked on at the crucifixion, they return to the tomb on Sunday morning to continue the burial rites, and there they meet the risen Lord who charges them with announcing the good news to the other disciples (*Friends of God and Prophets,* pp. 147, 148). Mary of Magdala, states Johnson, is "an apostolic leader who helps develop the gospel message and continues Jesus' preaching once he is gone" (ibid., p. 150).

In his novel Brown presupposes that Jesus intended to found an earthly royal dynasty. By identifying the church with such a royal dynasty he ignores the statement Jesus made to Pilate, "My kingdom is not from this world" (John 18:36). Entrusted by Jesus with the news that he was alive, Mary Magdalene achieved importance as a leader in the early church. Brown rails against the church for "demeaning the goddess" and trying to "smear" Mary's name, but in fact it's Brown who demeans her. He ignores her true importance and instead tries to domesticate her by attributing her significance merely to her supposed sexual relationship with a man.

53. We've often thought of Mary Magdalene as the sinful woman who repented, was forgiven by Jesus, and became his faithful follower. But Brown says that the church made her into a prostitute as part of a "smear campaign" to diminish her importance. What's the truth here?

We have already seen (Q. 33) that women were important leaders among the first Christians. As long as the early church remained a little minority group on the fringes of society, it continued to be "countercultural"—that is, it went against the prevailing norms of the day in many of its attitudes and actions, which included acknowledging women's leadership in an era that did not take women seriously in such a context. At that time Christians were grouped into local communities centered in house churches, in which women leaders were accepted because they often headed the households in which the community met for worship. Once Christianity began to emerge into the mainstream of society in the Roman Empire, however, in order to survive and to preserve its credibility the church tended increasingly to conform to prevalent social norms—which entailed making concessions where the expected role of women in a male-dominated society was concerned.

Despite Brown's assertions, Constantine is not to be blamed. Not only did this process predate the Edict of Milan (see Q. 22), but neither Constantine nor anyone else at that time made a conscious decision to inaugurate a "smear campaign" against Mary Magdalene.

54. Then how did Mary Magdalene come to be identified as a prostitute?

This resulted from the conflation, or combining, of several women from the Gospels and church history into one because of some salient characteristics they shared. Here's what happened:

The Gospels identify Mary Magdalene as a woman from whom Jesus had cast out seven demons (Mark 16:9; Luke 8:2).

The figure of Mary of Bethany, sister of Martha and Lazarus, appears in the Gospels of Luke and John. These two sisters and their brother were very close friends of Jesus. Luke portrays Mary in the supreme act of discipleship (which means "learner")—sitting at Jesus' feet listening to him speak (10:38–42). John recounts how, on Jesus' last visit to their home before his crucifixion, Mary anointed him: she "took a pound of costly perfume made of pure nard, anointed Jesus' feet, and wiped them with her hair" (John 12:3).

Further, the Synoptic Gospels (Matt 26:6–13; Mark 14:3–9; Luke 7:36–50) each tell the story of a woman with an alabaster jar filled with an expensive ointment, who approaches Jesus while he dines at the home of a leading Pharisee (named as Simon the Leper in Matthew and Luke). Luke identifies the woman as "a sinner" (7:37) and Jesus tells his host that the woman's sins, "'which were many,'" have been forgiven, and thus she "'has shown great love'" (7:47).

This sinful woman may have been further combined with the woman caught in adultery (John 8:2–11) and thus identified as a prostitute. Yet, the prostitute label may have definitively come not from a biblical woman but from another woman in church history who is, surprisingly, overlooked by scholars in this context, the fifth-century saint Mary of Egypt. In her early life Mary of Egypt actually was a harlot, not for need of money but, as she later told the monk Zosimas, "out of insatiable desire." Then one day, having joined a huge number of pilgrims in Jerusalem who were celebrating the feast of the Exaltation of the Cross, Mary was prevented by some force from entering the church. At that point, with waves of self-knowledge and remorse sweeping over her, she begged for forgiveness for her sins and was then able to enter the church. Mary spent the rest of her life as a desert solitary beyond the Jordan River. We know her story from Zosimas, who was sent to her toward the end of her life, when she had been in the desert for forty-seven years.

It's easy to see how details from St. Mary of Egypt's story may have brought her into the distinguished company of women that made up the popular image of Mary Magdalene. She was a repentant sinner who "watered the earth with [her] tears," just as the penitent woman washed Jesus' feet with her tears. Like Mary Magdalene, Mary of Egypt became a teacher, sharing her wisdom with the surprised monk Zosimas, who never expected to meet this humble, weather-beaten woman when the Lord directed him to go into the desert to find wisdom. Most importantly, St. Mary of Egypt's personal qualities of honesty, courage, and freedom recall Mary Magdalene as she stood by Jesus at the moment of his supreme sacrifice and then, on Easter, as she proclaimed to his disciples the "impossible" news that he had risen.

55. What were the important characteristics that caused all these women to be combined into the popular conception of Mary Magdalene?

They were especially the following:

Anointing. The anointing story in the Synoptic Gospels and John's story of Mary of Bethany anointing Jesus are so similar, it is easy to see how Mary of Bethany could have been identified with the anonymous woman of the Synoptics. How did Mary Magdalene enter the mix?

Sins forgiven. First, Luke introduces Mary Magdalene immediately after the story of the anointing by the sinful woman—"Mary, called Magdalene, from whom seven demons had gone out" (Luke 8:2). Although the mention of "demons" in the New Testament healing stories may well have referred to physical or mental illnesses, Luke's juxtaposition of these two stories may possibly have suggested that Mary's "demons" were sins, or at least some forms of subjection to evil forces.

Love. Undoubtedly the most important feature common to these women is that they showed great love: Luke's sinful woman, Mary of Bethany, and Mary of Magdala.

This conflation took place gradually, over the course of centuries, and it originally took place *in the popular imagination.* It did not result, in the first instance, from a deliberate, conscious plan conceived by the institutional church. In fact, the greatest of the church fathers in the third to fifth centuries—the Greek theologian Origen, along with Sts. Ambrose, Jerome, and Augustine—maintained that these were three separate women. Taking its cue from Origen, the Greek Church has always retained the women's separate identities. In the Western Church, however, the identities became conflated so that by the time of Pope Gregory I (St. Gregory the Great, ca. 540–604), the combination into a single woman identified as Mary of Magdala had been firmly established. Gregory may well have had pastoral reasons for equating Mary's "seven demons" with the "seven capital sins," but what's important is that he was reflecting and crystallizing what had been developing in popular devotion for centuries and not deliberately attempting to slander Mary of Magdala.

A true slandering of Mary Magdalene's reputation, born of the conflation of the different figures from scripture, was perpetrated closer to our own time, not by the official church, nor in the popular imagination, but by the so-called "visions" of the nineteenth-century German mystic Anne Catherine Emmerich—who was also the source of the anti-Semitic material adopted by Mel Gibson for his film *The Passion of the Christ*. These scurrilous visions, which dwell on Mary Magdalene's sinful life and which claim, for example, that she was "engaged in love affairs" as early as the age of nine, are best dismissed as the product of a lurid imagination. Unfortunately, they have undoubtedly misled many well-meaning persons who trusted them as a source of information about a beloved saint.

56. Then where did Dan Brown get the notion of deliberate smear tactics on the part of the church?

Brown borrows the accusation of a conscious effort by the church to slander Mary Magdalene from Margaret Starbird, who, as we've already noted, hardly commands respect as a reputable scholar. True to form, Starbird claims that the identification of Mary Magdalene as a prostitute must stem from the similarity of the anointing at Bethany to the ritual practices of sacred priestesses or temple "prostitutes" in Roman goddess cults *(The Woman with the Alabaster Jar)*. She and others of her ilk consistently overlook Luke's sinful woman and John's woman caught in adultery as contributing to the identification of Mary Magdalene as a prostitute.

The great irony is that Brown, for all his accusations against the church for denigrating Mary Magdalene, does precisely that by reducing her to someone defined solely by her alleged sexual relationship to a man and her biological reproductive role.

57. How do some theologians today view the identification of Mary Magdalene as a prostitute?

Feminist scholars such as Elizabeth Johnson and Rosemary Ruether deplore the way Mary Magdalene has been devalued over the centuries from respected leader in the early church to reformed prostitute. They point out, rightly, that this picture of her is not at all faithful to scripture. Johnson goes so far as to maintain that the devaluing of Mary Magdalene from one who occupied a "pivotal role at the foundation" of the church *(Friends of God and Prophets,* p. 164) to a repentant prostitute is an ethical issue because it involves a deep untruth.

Among the reasons these scholars offer for why this could have happened is the church's emergence into the mainstream of public life, in which women played lesser roles. As a consequence of this, the early memories of the prominent women leaders of the church faded (or were suppressed?). But what to do with a woman as outstanding as Mary Magdalene? Her memory refused to die completely. And so, these scholars claim, she was "reinvented" as a repentant sinner, a prostitute, by being conflated with several other women in the Gospels.

The conflation of several persons into one because of shared characteristics is gradual and usually not deliberate (see Q. 54), and thus it's likely that the entrance of St. Mary of Egypt into the conflation mix is overlooked by scholars who want to contend that the identification of Mary Magdalene as prostitute was deliberate. At any rate, even if the arguments of these scholars are correct, Mary Magdalene would have been "demoted" to a prostitute in order to obscure her original role as prominent leader of the early church and not, as Dan Brown contends, to cover up the "fact" that she was Jesus' wife and mother of his child.

58. Can there be any other factors that may have contributed to the gradual identification of this loving, loyal woman as a sinner?

Yes. It's likely that the process of conflation reflects an unconscious need for women to have an archetype, or icon, with whom they can identify: a sinful woman (though not necessarily a prostitute), yet redeemed and loved by Christ. If we acknowledge that we are all sinners, then why is the fact that Mary Magdalene has been regarded as a repentant sinner necessarily a negative? St. Peter was a sinner. He begged Jesus, "Go away from me, Lord, for I am a sinful man!" (Luke 5:8), and he denied Jesus at a critical moment when Jesus most needed support from a friend. St. Paul, who began by persecuting the church, ended up as one of its greatest apostles whose preaching and evangelizing were crucial to the spread of Christianity throughout the known world. St. Matthew, who was a tax collector—an occupation then considered to be among the dregs of society—was called by Jesus to be one of the Twelve; and tradition associates him with the writing of one of the canonical Gospels.

Stories like these—dare we call them biblical "success stories"?—give hope to us who acknowledge our sinfulness, and they embody Jesus' promise of heaven rejoicing over a repentant sinner. If the mother of Jesus has tended at times to be elevated and ritually divinized to the point where an ordinary woman could neither identify with nor hope to imitate her, then the very human Mary Magdalene, as archetype of a wounded yet redeemed woman, filled the gap. For the female psyche it was almost necessary that a forgiven woman sinner be raised up as a counter-image to the sinless "spotless virgin" mother of Jesus.

Even the great eleventh-century theologian St. Anselm of Canterbury wrote a prayer to Mary Magdalene in which he finds solace in her image as a repentant sinner. Identifying with Mary in her sinfulness—note how this transcends gender!—Anselm can focus on the mercy and forgiveness she received and thus derive the hope that he will receive the same.

Conversion stories have always been and will always be inspiring and encouraging. If we celebrate the conversion of St. Paul and, indeed, raise this event to the level of a liturgical feast, then the image of Mary Magdalene as a repentant sinner, while scripturally inaccurate, need not be unrelievedly negative.

59. How can we honor Mary Magdalene today? What qualities make her an appropriate object of devotion for contemporary Catholics?

In her book *Mary of Magdala* Mary Thompson has this to say: "Christians today do well to study Mary of Magdala as a leader whose total devotion and self-assurance enabled her to act upon her own convictions without concern about opposition, hostility or improbability. She provided the example of an individual who stood tall for what she believed and for the Lord whom she loved."

Mary Magdalene was a woman of conviction and a woman of action. She didn't waste time on verbal polemic—she simply did what needed to be done.

She had an extraordinary openness to the seemingly impossible. In John's Gospel she starts out by looking for a dead body in order to complete the decent burial rites for it. But suddenly she is confronted with the awesome truth of the resurrection—a possibility she hadn't considered at all—and without completely understanding what has happened, she believes; and her faith is so strong, she has no problem with announcing to others this news that, in any other context, would appear quite preposterous.

As Mary Magdalene's faith is strong, so, too, is her love. It's easy to imagine her as an exuberant, physically demonstrative person; in John's Gospel, when she recognizes the risen Jesus upon hearing him call her name, she must have tried to embrace him, because Jesus cautions her not to touch him. In the First Reading for the liturgy of her feast day, the church does not hesitate to put before us an excerpt from the Song of Songs, a heartrending poem of intimacy in which the lover single-mindedly and undauntedly goes in search of "him whom [her] heart loves."

As Thompson observes, "The gospel portrait of Mary of Magdala provides an inspiring paradigm for true leadership which is not gender dependent." Women and men alike can derive inspiration and encouragement from the story of Mary Magdalene, a faith-filled, loving, loyal, and indomitable leader in the early church.

SEVEN

THE HOLY GRAIL

60. How did the story of the Holy Grail get started?

The Grail has been a recurrent image in Western literature for eight centuries. An excellent resource on it is by Richard Barber, a recognized medieval historian, who published a thorough, scholarly study titled *The Holy Grail* (2004).

The Grail legend began toward the end of the twelfth century when a poet named Chrétien de Troyes composed a romance that he named *The Story of the Grail*. In fact, it is really the story of the adventures of Perceval and his quest to achieve knighthood. His quest leads him to a ruined castle occupied by a wounded nobleman called the Fisher King, and it is here that the Grail appears for the first time. The story breaks off—it has been left incomplete—and there is no resolution.

After Chrétien, several other writers, all working within about three or four decades of Chrétien's version, took up the tale. It is difficult to assign them an exact chronology. One important author was Robert de Boron, who wrote his *Romance of the History of the Grail* between 1200 and 1210. Robert de Boron takes the story back to the time of Jesus and relates the Grail story to the Gospels both canonical and apocryphal. He introduces Joseph of Arimathea as a key figure in the story. Having been given the vessel in which Jesus broke bread at the Last Supper, Joseph uses it to collect the blood from Jesus' wounds when his body is taken down from the cross. After the resurrection, Jesus appears to Joseph and commissions him to celebrate Mass in remembrance of his crucifixion. Despite its title, Robert de Boron's tale is less like a romance than like then-current lives of the saints and contemporary French versions of the apocryphal Gospels.

The identity of the Grail as the vessel in which Jesus' blood was gathered at his crucifixion appears also in a romance called

Perlesvaus (another version of the name "Perceval"), roughly contemporary with Robert de Boron's version. The details of this story unfold in events at King Arthur's court. Some time in the 1220s another connection between the Grail and Christ's passion is made in *The Quest of the Holy Grail*. This story, which has Sir Lancelot as its protagonist, depicts a Grail liturgy in which Christ himself emerges from the Grail and gives out communion to the assembled Grail knights.

Perhaps the best-known version of the Grail story, because the composer Richard Wagner based his music drama *Parsifal* on it (see Q. 62), is Wolfram von Eschenbach's *Parzival,* written between 1210 and 1220. Wolfram's story is very much taken up with the personal quest and destiny of the knight Parzival (or Perceval).

61. How do these various authors describe the Grail? What, actually, *is* the Holy Grail?

This is important in view of Brown's allegation, expressed as certainty in his novel, that the Grail is to be identified with Mary Magdalene. What *is* the Grail? In fact, the various medieval authors of Grail stories provide no unanimous answer to this question. The word itself was in current use in twelfth-century French, and it meant a platter or dish. Chrétien's Grail—which he calls "such a holy thing" but does not define its shape—is made of pure gold and set with precious stones. Presumably it is some kind of vessel or dish, because Perceval is meant to ask who "is served from" the Grail. In Chrétien the word has no hidden meanings or religious connotations; Chrétien's Grail is precisely what he says it is. The Grail's "powerful religious connotations" (see Barber, p. 95) developed after Chrétien: in subsequent works it "has become part of the central drama of the Christian faith—the Crucifixion of Jesus" (Barber, p. 93).

In the anonymous *First Continuation* of Chrétien's tale, the Grail miraculously feeds the assembled company, just as in

Wolfram's *Parzival* people are fed from the Grail at a sumptuous banquet, although Wolfram's Grail is a transcendent, beautiful stone. A hermit tells Parzival that every Good Friday a dove comes down from heaven with a small white wafer that it leaves at the stone, and from this wafer—clearly meant to represent a communion host—the Grail derives its power to feed.

In *The Quest of the Holy Grail* the Grail is an instrument of healing: upon seeing it, Sir Gawain—and later Perceval and Sir Lancelot's brother Ector—recover from severe wounds.

Thus it's clear that, in the various versions of the Grail story, the Grail assumes different shapes and functions.

62. So, does the Grail have anything to do with Mary Magdalene or the lost sacred feminine?

No. Brown makes much of identifying the Grail with a chalice, to which he attributes feminine symbolism. It would appear, however, that the only version of medieval Grail literature that specifically equates the Grail with a chalice is Manessier's *Third Continuation* of Chrétien's story (possibly written between 1210 and 1220), and even there it's not in the text but in an illustration in a late thirteenth-century French manuscript that shows the Grail in the form of a large covered chalice.

While Joseph of Arimathea figures prominently as "Grail keeper" in a number of versions, no mention is made of Mary Magdalene, much less even a hint of a royal bloodline of descendants of Mary Magdalene and Jesus. And Brown's suggestion that Wagner's music drama *Parsifal* is a "tribute" to such a bloodline (p. 390) would have surprised no one more than Wagner himself. In fact, Barber (*Holy Grail,* p. 284) argues that, despite its Christian imagery, *Parsifal* is not a specifically Christian work. The notion of Kundry, the female protagonist, representing Mary Magdalene is well off the mark: her "love scene" with Parsifal is an attempted seduction meant to destroy him and to get the Grail into the hands of an evil magician, hardly the stuff of a loving marriage.

Brown dramatically introduces (from his "historians," see Q. 1) the idea that *san greal* (Holy Grail) is actually a misreading of *sang real* (royal blood). However, as Barber demonstrates—and he also cites Lisa Jefferson, an accredited scholar of Arthurian literature—*sang real* is a misreading of *san greal* and not vice versa. The original meaning of the word, combined with its usual identification in Grail literature as some sort of vessel or something from which people are fed, shows that *san greal* is the correct reading.

Brown's association of the Grail with the Knights Templar is also spurious. As Barber argues (*Holy Grail,* p. 179), the *templeisen,* or keepers of the Grail in Wolfram's *Parzival,* are not the same as the Knights Templar, who had "a very low profile" at the time; and he cites evidence that German nobles of the late Middle Ages didn't equate the Templars with the *templeisen.*

The adventures involving the Grail are supposed to have taken place in the British Isles, in the circle of King Arthur and his famous knights: Perceval, Lancelot, Galahad, and so forth. It's possible that Chrétien got the idea for his story from a Welsh source. Also, an ancient legend connecting Joseph of Arimathea with England claims that he sometimes traveled there on business and that the young Jesus accompanied him on one of his trips. This story gave rise to William Blake's poem "Jerusalem," familiar and beloved in its musical setting by C. Hubert Parry.

63. There seems to be considerable variety among the details in the several Grail stories. What important features do the different versions have in common, especially from a Christian perspective?

Because the best-known Grail stories—the Lancelot cycle and Wolfram's *Parzival*—involve a quest for the Grail itself, the "Grail" in popular parlance has evolved into a metaphor for an elusive "something" for which one is searching. Even a book on the Ivory-billed Woodpecker, published in 2005 shortly after the exciting discovery of this bird that had been presumed extinct, was titled *The Grail Bird*!

Yet, the Grail romances make clear that the Grail is no mere prize to possess. In some versions not even the Grail itself but a lance—often identified as the spear that pierced Christ's side on the cross—is the object of the quest. Regardless of the object, however, its attainment is never an end in itself; rather, it's only the beginning, because the attainment of the object of the quest, whether Grail or lance, entails *service*. The one who succeeds in the quest becomes the Grail-keeper, which implies responsibilities to and in the Grail community: Wolfram's Parzival, for example, is destined to become head of the dynasty that *serves* the Grail. As Jesus reminds each of his followers, "Whoever wishes to be great among you must be your servant" (Matt 20:26). Note, too, the importance of compassion in the quest: Perceval must *ask a question* in order that the wounded king might be healed; he must show compassion by expressing his concern in the form of a question. In his music drama Wagner portrays Parsifal being "made wise through compassion."

The quest motif thus becomes a metaphor for the Christian life. It is a journey, a life pilgrimage, undertaken by those who sell all to obtain the "pearl of great price" that Jesus speaks of, which is the kingdom of God. Thus the Grail is, appropriately, closely bound up with Christ's passion. The adventures undertaken and wounds sustained by the Grail knights mirror, in their small way, Jesus' sufferings on the cross. Just as Jesus did not attain the glory of Easter without first undergoing the agony of Good Friday, so too the Grail heroes could not succeed in their quest without the hardships and tests they endured. The different versions that followed Chrétien's Grail romance abound with motifs associated with the passion: The Grail is a vessel in which Christ's blood is collected; the idea of collecting Christ's blood from his crucifixion goes back at least to 1125, from which year dates a gospel book with a miniature illumination of Jesus being taken down from the cross. Barber comments that this is "the first evidence in Western Europe of a tradition that the blood of Christ was collected when his body was taken down from the cross" (*Holy Grail,* p. 123). Joseph of Arimathea, who in the Gospels assumes responsibility for burying Jesus' body, becomes the Grail's guardian and even a priest. Wolfram specifically associates the Grail with Good Friday, an idea of which Wagner makes much in his music drama, in which all of creation joins in the commemoration of this sacred day.

In Wolfram a white wafer is a significant part of the Grail story and provides explicit evidence of eucharistic associations in the legend. The Grail feeds people, and does so sumptuously, just as Christ nourishes his believers in the eucharistic banquet. The Eucharist as a source of healing is reflected in the Grail's power to heal; there is an interesting parallel between the Grail's healing of various knights *when they looked at it,* and the healing of those bitten by serpents when they looked upon a bronze serpent fashioned and lifted up by Moses during the exodus. The Christian tradition often views the bronze serpent as a "type," or foreshadowing, of Christ, who also was lifted up—on the cross.

It's no coincidence that the Grail romances developed at the same time as popular and theological focus on the Eucharist was increasing; this was a period that culminated in the great eucharistic hymns of St. Thomas Aquinas, which we still sing today.

A quest for the precious kingdom of God, a relic of the saving passion of Christ, a reflection of the Eucharist—the Grail is all these things. It's unfortunate that Dan Brown has followed the authors of spurious "histories" in using this beautiful image to miseducate and mislead.

EIGHT

THE PRIORY OF SION, KNIGHTS TEMPLAR, AND FREEMASONS

64. According to Dan Brown, the Priory of Sion was founded by Godefroi de Bouillon in 1099 to protect the secret of Christ's lineage and to preserve the tradition of goddess worship (p. 113). Does this organization really exist?

Brown's version of the Priory of Sion, with its millennium-long pedigree and alleged Merovingian connections that persist even to this day, is another figment of Brown's favorite "sources," notably the authors of *Holy Blood, Holy Grail*. It doesn't exist in that form and never has. Its alleged founder, Godefroi de Bouillon (ca. 1060–1100), was not a French king but the duke of Lower Lorraine. One of the heroes of the First Crusade, Godefroi led in the capture of Jerusalem from the Muslims in 1099, and for his exploits was named first Latin ruler in Palestine. He refused the title "king" and instead styled himself "Protector of the Holy Sepulchre." After his death his younger brother Baldwin became king of Jerusalem.

This was the age of romance, chivalry, legends, and sagas, and Godefroi became the hero of many such works; his story was even conflated with the "Swan Knight" legend that eventually formed the basis of Richard Wagner's opera *Lohengrin*. He was known for his piety, and religious motives had inspired him to join the Crusades. He never involved himself with anything as esoteric as the promotion of goddess worship. Godefroi's "connection" with the esoteric twentieth-century Priory of Sion (see Q. 65) originated in the 1930s with an Italian esoteric thinker named Julius Evola, who happened to admire Godefroi. Evola was influential on Pierre Plantard and others in France who were busy fabricating their false "Jesus bloodline."

65. Is the Priory of Sion totally fictitious, then, or does it have any basis in reality?

There was a real Priory of Sion, but it was founded in the twentieth century, and the notion of the Holy Grail as a "bloodline" came from fraudulent documents written by this group, which actually was an extreme right-wing anti-Semitic French sect.

This organization has forebears going back to nineteenth-century France, where continuous political turmoil that lasted until the mid-twentieth century spawned the formation of numerous groups that belonged either to the far right or to the republican cause, and many of these groups had esoteric interests. With the spread of anti-Semitism in Europe during the 1930s, this became part of the ideology of the right-wing groups. It was at this time that Pierre Plantard rose to prominence. An avowed anti-Semite and Nazi sympathizer, Plantard founded several organizations in succession designed to advance his agenda, which eventually included his phony claim to be descended from the Merovingians (see Q. 48).

In 1956 Plantard founded the Priory of Sion, which not only continued promoting his right-wing agenda but also added a good deal of esoterica to the mix. This is when he began to forge his claim about the existence of a "secret" about Jesus' "bloodline" and about an alleged connection between his organization and the Knights Templar (see Q. 67). The false claims were supported by the fabrication of phony documents that were then placed in key French libraries, and by the creation of a fake genealogy for Plantard linking him to ancient bloodlines.

Since the organization dates back only as far as 1956, it is impossible for its membership to have included such names as Botticelli, Leonardo da Vinci, Sir Isaac Newton, and Victor Hugo.

66. So, was there ever a Priory of Sion officially associated with the church as a religious organization?

No. A church named Hagia Sion, built on Mount Zion, was burnt by Persian invaders in AD 614, rebuilt, and then partially destroyed again in AD 1009. So when the Crusaders arrived in Jerusalem in 1099, Hagia Sion was in ruins. In the twelfth century the Crusaders built a new church over part of these ruins, which they named St. Mary of Zion to commemorate the tradition that Mary had lived there after the resurrection of Jesus. There were priests (called canons) who served this church, but there is no evidence that they were connected in any way to the Knights Templar. The church of St. Mary was destroyed by the Muslims in 1219, the priests moved to Sicily, and their "order" disbanded in 1617, when its members joined the Society of Jesus.

67. Who are the Knights Templar? Were they really the military arm of the Priory of Sion, as Dan Brown claims (p. 356)?

The Knights Templar were one of the two principal military religious orders to be formed during the course of the Crusades. Thus they were, in a sense, a military arm of the church, not of the Priory of Sion. The First Crusade—during which the Crusaders successfully captured Jerusalem in 1099—resulted in the founding of several Western Christian states in what is now the Middle East and Turkey; consequently, the assumption that it was now safe to travel to the Holy Land caused pilgrims to stream to these sites in vast numbers. The presumed safety was an illusion, however, especially for pilgrims traveling between Constantinople and Jerusalem, and in 1118 over three hundred pilgrims were massacred by the Muslims. In addition, Jerusalem itself would soon be threatened with recapture by the Muslims. So the existence of a permanent military presence on the pilgrim route (the Templars constructed forts along the way) and in the city itself was necessary for the continuation of a Christian presence.

In 1119 or 1120 Hugh de Payens and eight knights banded together in order to ensure the safe passage of pilgrims to and from the Holy Land, and to protect the holy places in Jerusalem. King Baldwin of Jerusalem welcomed the knights—pilgrimages were, after all, the main source of income in his kingdom—and gave them living quarters in a wing of his palace. Thus they were known as the Poor Knights of Christ and of the Temple of Solomon, or the "Knights Templar" or "Templars," because they were first quartered on the grounds of Solomon's Temple. In 1128 the Council of Troyes granted them official approval as a religious order and gave them their formal rule, which was drawn up along Cistercian lines by the influential St. Bernard of Clairvaux. The Templars had ranks of knights, sergeants, squires, and chaplains; they took monastic vows, were enjoined to dress simply, and were expressly forbidden any contact with women. It was probably this latter rule that later caused homosexuality to be added to the trumped-up charges against them.

68. So, the Templars were vowed religious as well as soldiers. Why would a soldier want to become a member of a religious order?

Vow-taking was nothing new to soldiers in the Middle Ages. When a soldier enlisted for the First Crusade in 1096, he took a religious vow to stay with the army until it achieved its goal, the capture of Jerusalem from the Muslims. Failure to keep the vow—through desertion, for example—would result in excommunication. What the church hoped to achieve by this was the formation of an army disciplined by the knowledge of its solemn promise, but also oriented toward the spiritual goal of the recovery of the holy places from people who had plundered them and were preventing Christians from visiting them.

Religious fervor was the order of the day. In the eleventh century the Augustinian, Cistercian, and Carthusian monks were founded, soon to be followed by the Franciscans and Dominicans in the 1200s. Many other orders were founded as well, some of which would prove to be heretical. So it was natural that crusading soldiers often desired to go beyond the temporary achievement of a finite goal, but rather commit their lives to the protection of Christian pilgrims.

The other principal military order to emerge from the Crusades were the Knights Hospitaller, who had both a medical and military wing. The Templars and the Hospitallers were principally responsible for continuing the crusading spirit, until Acre—modern-day 'Akko in Israel, which had been the capital of the Crusader Kingdom in 1104—fell to the Muslims in 1291.

69. Why did the Crusades happen in the first place?

Ever since the seventh century, Jerusalem had been under the control of Muslims, either Arabian or Egyptian. Access to the Christian holy places, while restricted, was still permitted. Unfortunately, early in the eleventh century, the Turks, under the Caliph Hakim, had taken over Jerusalem and began a ten-year pogrom against Christians, restricting their movement, mandating the wearing of distinctive clothing, etc. Church property began to be confiscated, crosses were burnt, and little mosques built on church roofs. In 1009 Hakim ordered the destruction of the Church of the Holy Sepulchre in Jerusalem and, by 1014, some 30,000 churches had been burnt or pillaged. Christian pilgrims, who had peacefully coexisted with Arab rulers of Jerusalem, now found themselves harassed by the Turks, and reports and rumors of beatings, robberies, and molestations began to filter back to Europe, creating an atmosphere of collective outrage suitable to the beginning of a war, similar to that experienced after the news of Pearl Harbor or the destruction of the World Trade Towers in September 2001. You do not get 50,000 men to march a distance the equivalent of New York to California, over several years, unless they are very angry about something.

70. Did the Templars discover documents in the cellar of the Temple of Solomon, as Brown claims (p. 158)?

Although they inhabited the Temple Mount for a time — more for its central location and high ground than for any theological reason—the Templars were far more concerned with protecting Christian buildings, such as the Church of the Holy Sepulchre. There is no historical evidence that any secret documents existed in the crypt of the Temple, which had been destroyed in AD 70 by the Roman Emperor Titus. Why documents pertaining to the foundation of early Christianity would have been found in the crypt of the Jewish Temple is a question that Dan Brown does not attempt to answer. But besides this obvious lapse of logic, there is no basis in history for any claim that the Knights Templar possessed secret information found on the Temple grounds, all of it detrimental to the traditional Christian story. It stretches the bounds of belief that the Templars would have continued to fight doggedly for centuries, and with great loss, in order to preserve Christian sites that such documents would have ridiculed.

71. Is it true, as Brown suggests (p. 145), that the equal-armed cross adopted by the Knights Templar predated Christianity by 1,500 years and was originally a pagan sex symbol, signifying the union of male and female?

Crosses did predate Christianity, although it is still not known what their significance was, whether they were used for purposes of ownership and identification ("x marks the spot") or in worship. The Egyptian Ankh, or cross with a loop on the top, was a hieroglyph that signified life. The Coptic (Egyptian Christian) Church used it extensively, especially in tomb decorations.

In addition to adopting a white robe similar to that worn by the Cistercian monks, the Templars also adopted a red Greek or "Maltese" cross, a cross with four equal flared arms. Other military orders adopted the "Jerusalem" cross with four equal arms, but with four smaller crosses (also with equal arms) intermixed. This symbolized the five wounds of Christ: the nails in his two hands and two feet, and the crown of thorns. In addition, many Eastern Christian churches, such as Hagia Sophia in Constantinople, and even Western Christian churches—including the present St. Peter's

Basilica in Rome, which was begun in the year 1503—were built in the shape of a Greek cross.

72. Were Christian churches constructed by the Templars deliberately round in defiance of the traditional cruciform architecture of the church, as Brown claims (p. 339), and was their roundness a symbol of the sun?

Dan Brown wants to have it several ways. He wants the Templars to build round churches because the round shape is pagan and not cruciform, but then he says that they built Rosslyn Chapel in Scotland in the shape of the Temple of Solomon in Jerusalem—a large rectangular building.

Most of the churches built by the Templars were, in fact, not round at all, although their most distinctive churches, such as the Temple in London, are round or octagonal. Despite what Brown claims, this roundness is patterned after the Church of the Holy Sepulchre in Jerusalem, which can hardly be called a temple for sun worship.

Round churches were hardly unknown in early and medieval Christianity. In the fifth century in Rome, a secular building—a shopping center, it is thought—was transformed into a Christian place of worship, the Church of San Stefano Rotondo (which means "in the round"), as it still remains. The even more famous Pantheon in Rome was easily adaptable for Christian worship. The Church of San Vitale in Ravenna, built in the sixth century, is another example of a "rounded" or octagonal Christian building.

73. What became of the Templars?

In the nearly two hundred years of their existence the Templars amassed considerable property, both in the Mideast and in Europe, and great wealth, which was deposited in their "Temples" and banks in London and Paris. The wealth was acquired via estates and properties given them by the royalty and nobility in Europe, and through their ability to collect and transport bullion safely between Europe and the Holy Land, so that they were used as bankers.

The Templars were disbanded because King Philip IV of France wanted their wealth. It really is as simple as that. In the days before property or income was taxed regularly, the leveling of a tax could be political suicide. Thus, rather than risk revolt, dissent, or civil war, kings would confiscate soft targets, such as indigent religious houses. In 1535, King Henry VIII of England did something similar. He needed money desperately, and so, through his ingenious lieutenant Thomas Cromwell, he concocted the nationalization of all monastic property in England and Wales on the trumped-up charges that the monasteries were corrupt. This saved Henry from taxing his people and eliminated the religious orders' potential (and real) opposition to his marital projects. Thus the Templars were especially vulnerable, because they were quite wealthy and their real raison d'être—the continuation of the Crusades—no longer existed.

74. So, it was the king of France and not the pope who dissolved the Templars, unlike what Brown states (p. 338)?

Pope Clement V had practically nothing to do with it. The "Friday the thirteenth" episode mentioned by Brown (p. 338) was perpetrated not by the church, as he claims, but by King Philip IV of France. On that date in 1307 Philip had every Templar in France arrested and their property sequestered on trumped-up charges of heresy, homosexuality, pagan practices, and so forth, because he wanted their wealth. A month later, under pressure from Philip, Pope Clement V ordered the arrest of Templars everywhere.

In 1312 the Templars were suppressed and their wealth confiscated by the state. Many Templars were executed and imprisoned—by the state, not by the church—and in 1314 their last Grand Master was burned at the stake. The notion of dead

Templar bodies floating down the Tiber River in Rome is another Dan Brown invention (p. 338). Pope Clement V never saw Rome since he was born, raised, elected and reigned as pope, and died— all in France. So, even if he were executing Templars, he would not have been sending their bodies down the Tiber.

75. Why did the pope allow the Templars to be disbanded? Is it not true, then, that the pope wanted to suppress the Templars' secret about Jesus and Mary Magdalene?

The pope did not have much choice about the disbanding of the Templars. He was virtually a prisoner of the French king. In 1305, when he was elected to be pope, he was the Archbishop of Bordeaux. He was crowned in Lyons and settled in Avignon in 1309. The curia became nervous about returning to Rome because of the disturbed condition of Italy, antipapal risings in Rome, and the growing need for French support and security. For the next one hundred years, the French dominated the church, mostly because of pressure (financial and military) from the French crown. This is known as the Babylonian Captivity, and it was ended when Catherine of Siena persuaded Pope Gregory XI to return to Rome (see Q. 35).

As an example of the French king's hold on the papacy, Clement created ten cardinals in 1305, of whom one was English and nine French. As the papal court remained in the bishop's palace in Avignon, a vast fortified palace housing an elaborate administrative machinery was gradually established, and this added to the curia's reluctance to move back to Rome. Of the 134 cardinals created by the Avignon popes, 112 were French. Seventy percent of all the curial officials were French. This pattern was finally broken in the early 1400s.

The strong connection between the state and the church in the Middle Ages was much stronger than we realize. If a king was angry at the pope for whatever reason, he had considerable leverage to exact concessions from the papacy: he could threaten to dismiss religious orders, to confiscate church property, to remove clerical privileges such as exemption from taxation, and even to imprison certain highly placed clerics. When the Reformation threatened Scotland, Stuart kings demanded that their illegitimate sons be appointed abbots of various abbeys in Scotland, or they would join the Reformation. When Henry VIII did not get his way with his attempted divorce from Catherine of Aragon, he confiscated the property of every religious house in his realm. Popes had to be careful. So when the king of France said he wanted to disband the Templars, the pope, who was living under the king's hospitality, had little choice but to go along with this. It had nothing to do with the Templars' supposed secret knowledge about Jesus and Mary Magdalene that he wanted to eliminate; he agreed to the disbanding of the Templars because he did not have the courage or the means to stand up to the king of France.

76. Why do the Freemasons claim some connection to the Templars?

The Freemasons, who were not founded until the early 1700s, wanted to claim some credibility as an "ancient order," and so they fixed on a Catholic religious order that had actually existed but had been dissolved. This fascination with a medieval religious order also gave the Freemasons a "rite" and hierarchy, which could prove annoying to Rome. The person who first made the connection between the Templars and the Freemasons was Andrew Michael Ramsey (1696–1743), a Scotsman and the chancellor of the Grand Lodge in France.

When the Reformation put an end to the construction of cathedrals—especially in the British Isles where Roman Catholic cathedrals were simply appropriated by the Protestant religion or the State—masons began recruiting into their brotherhood "honorary" members who had nothing to do with the building trades. In the Middle Ages the mason's shed was known as a "lodge," and the founding of Freemasonry can be traced to 1717 in England with the founding of the Grand Lodge. Increasingly, Freemasons became anti-Catholic and anticlerical, and they adopted the beliefs of the Enlightenment with its emphasis on deism, naturalism, and rationalism. Adherents to non-Christian religions could be admitted to Masonic lodges and the mention of the name of Jesus Christ was forbidden, even though one imaginative Masonic historian claimed that Christ was himself a Master Mason!

The Roman Catholic Church condemned membership in Masonic organizations because of their religious ambiguity, their insistence on the taking of oaths, and their rituals, which often mirrored Roman Catholic liturgy. Masons had temples, used altars, wore vestments, and adopted some of the trappings of religious and chivalric orders, such as the Knights Templar. But the church was also suspicious of the secrecy of the various initiation rites and identification signs, such as handshakes and passwords, and would remain wary of any secret societies well into the twentieth century.

Masonic lodges today have become little more than charitable organizations, such as the "Ancient Arabic Order of the Nobles of the Mystic Shrine," popularly known as the Shriners, but the taint of their anti-Catholicism remains.

NINE

CHURCHES AND CHAPELS

77. Dan Brown asserts (p. 432) that Rosslyn Chapel in Scotland was built by the Knights Templar, who designed it "as an exact architectural blueprint" of the Temple of Solomon in Jerusalem. What is the history of Rosslyn Chapel? And is Brown's claim true?

No. Archaeological evidence through excavation of the site shows that the present structure was to be part of a larger cruciform structure and so would not have mirrored the Temple of Solomon at all. The most typical buildings erected by the Templars were round or polygonal, such as their Temple in London, and were copied after the Church of the Holy Sepulchre in Jerusalem, not after the Temple of Solomon.

Rosslyn Chapel is a small church about seven miles south of Edinburgh, Scotland, built by a Scottish noble family in the mid-fifteenth century—in other words, more than one hundred years after the Knights Templar had been disbanded. It was built as a "collegiate" chapel, which meant that it was funded by a secular source (the St. Clair or Sinclair family) and not a religious order, and its purpose was to provide funding for scholars, most of whom were clerics. Of the thirty-seven collegiate churches built in Scotland between 1406 and 1513, Rosslyn Chapel is unique (and well worth seeing) for the sheer amount of its stone carving; it simply abounds with gargoyles, carved pillars, bosses, ceiling decorations, and so forth. One sad story is recounted that an apprentice carved a pillar while the master mason was away, only to have the master mason return and slay the young apprentice for his effrontery. To this day, this pillar is known as the "Apprentice's Pillar."

78. Where does the name "Rosslyn" come from? Is it true that it's connected with a "Rose Line" that connects Rosslyn Chapel and Glastonbury Abbey in southwestern England?

The name "Rosslyn" actually comes from two Scottish words, "Ross" and "Lyn," that describe the geographical location of the chapel and nearby castle: on the *hill* above the *stream*. Brown's claim that the name has something to do with a longitudinal "Rose Line" between Rosslyn and Glastonbury is inaccurate. These two "Grail towns" are *not* on the same longitudinal line, but they're close enough for him to draw the connection. In fact, the concept of longitude was not even developed until long after Rosslyn Chapel was completed (see Q. 82).

79. What of Brown's descriptions of the architecture and art of Rosslyn Chapel (chapter 104)? Does the chapel contain non-Christian features?

There is a small burial vault under Rosslyn Chapel that still contains the bodies of the Sinclair family. It is accessible through an opening in the floor of the chapel. Brown's "massive" underground vault that supposedly contains revealing documents about early Christianity doesn't exist—a massive vault would never support the stone church above.

As far as stone stars carved into the chapel ceiling are concerned, the depiction of stars on the ceilings of chapels was very common in Christian architecture. In several sixth-century church buildings in Ravenna, stars cover the mosaic ceilings and symbolize the heavens. Christ is often depicted in early Christian art as sitting on a throne in the starry heavens. Even the ceiling of the Sistine Chapel, before Michelangelo decorated it, was originally frescoed with stars in a field of blue.

Finally, there are no lines on the floor of Rosslyn Chapel. As we see elsewhere (Q. 92), the Star of David did not become a universally recognized Jewish symbol until some four centuries after Rosslyn Chapel was built.

80. Why does Brown connect the Freemasons with Rosslyn Chapel?

Obviously, masons built this chapel. It is almost completely made of stone and bears the typical marks of masons, not only in the carvings themselves, but in anagrams carved into the stones, identifying the individual mason. But masons in 1450 were not the same as Masons of the seventeenth and eighteenth centuries. The anti-Catholicism of Masonic "lodges" only surfaced in the late sixteenth century, with the rise of Protestantism (see Q. 76). Guilds, or medieval unions, had been in the habit of sponsoring religious plays and displays. The dome of the cathedral in Florence was paid for by the Wool Guild. Morality plays and passion plays were sponsored by various guilds in England. Oftentimes the play would represent the particular craft of the guild. Thus, carpenters would fund a passion play that highlighted the carving of the cross on which Christ died, or stress the connection between the Cross of Christ and the tree of the Garden of Eden. The Wool Guild would sponsor a play that featured the Lamb of God. When the Reformation ended these customs, guilds needed to be de-Catholicized and transformed into tools for the spread of the Reformation. The masons led the way, recruiting members who were not necessarily involved in the stone and brick business but who were convinced Protestants.

The "Scottish Rite" Masonic Lodge is a good example. Members went through various degrees of a "hierarchy" and practiced various rituals to announce their loyalty to the organization. They also sought to attach themselves to a religious order that had been suppressed by Rome. Hence their relatively recent connection to the Knights Templar. None of this was known to the real masons of the fifteenth century. They had induction ceremonies, no doubt, and various levels of competence and achievement (master masons, masons, apprentices), but it was all directed toward their craft and had no antireligious overtones. So it is only by projecting relatively recent Masonic practices (or Freemasonry) back into the fifteenth century that people see a conspiracy.

81. Dan Brown mentions the Church of Saint-Sulpice as a rallying point for Grail legends and unorthodoxy (p. 88). Is this true?

Saint-Sulpice is a church in Paris built in the mid-seventeenth century over previous churches that date back at least to the ninth century. Brown's claim that it was built over the ruins of a temple to Isis is wishful thinking, but it would not have been unheard of for Christians to build on the ruins of ancient temples. The Dominican church of Santa Maria sopra Minerva in Rome literally and unashamedly announces that it was built over the Temple of Minerva. Several pagan temples in the Mediterranean world were transformed into Christian churches in the fourth century. Most notably, the Pantheon in Rome — the Temple to All the Gods — was eventually dedicated to All the Saints.

The driving force behind the construction of the current Church of Saint-Sulpice was the church's parish priest, Jean Jacques Olier (1608–57), who established Saint-Sulpice Seminary in Paris and founded the Sulpicians (after Saint-Sulpice), a group of secular priests whose mission was to run seminaries. The charge of "unorthodoxy" was leveled at the professors at Saint-Sulpice during the eighteenth-century Enlightenment, when many clerics, especially those in the cities, became interested in the ideals of freedom and democracy.

82. Dan Brown sees another "Rose Line" running through Saint-Sulpice. Is there one?

Dan Brown would almost have one believe that this metal strip — this "pagan astronomical device" — appeared magically in the floor (p. 105). Actually, there is a metal line running through the floor of the church that at one time represented the zero meridian (or longitude), when longitude was first established. (This measurement has since been moved to Greenwich, England). The incorporation of an astronomical measurement in the floor or fabric of a church has never been extraordinary or unusual. For one thing, Christian churches faced east, toward the rising sun, symbolic of the Son of God and resurrection. But, perhaps more importantly, because of the size of churches—which were often the tallest building in a town—astronomical measurements could best be made from the church. The cathedral in Bologna is a good example; its floor is covered with astronomical data. Dan Brown makes more of this line in Saint-Sulpice than it deserves. The establishment of longitude is relatively recent and cannot in any way be related to something elemental and pagan, despite Dan Brown's assertions.

TEN

OPUS DEI

83. On his celebrated "fact" page at the beginning of *The Da Vinci Code*, Dan Brown states that Opus Dei is a Catholic "sect." Is Opus Dei a sect?

A sect, at least in the Catholic tradition, is usually a schismatic group that has broken away from the larger institution over some grievance about liturgical practice, disciplinary decision, or theological belief. While some or most of the church's practices and beliefs are retained, the sect will function with its own rules. A modern example of a sect is the Lefebvrists, whose grievance with the church is the liturgical reform of Vatican II, and whose members celebrate the Mass in the Tridentine Rite, commonly known as the old Latin Mass. They are schismatic, but derive from the church through their founder, Archbishop Marcel Lefebvre. Another sect, founded in the United States, was the Polish National Catholic Church, begun in the nineteenth century as a protest against the domination of the Irish-American hierarchy. This sect has since been reconciled to Rome.

Opus Dei was founded in 1928 in Spain in order to move its members to a greater integration of their faith with their daily lives. Today, Opus Dei has 83,000 laypeople and 2,000 priests worldwide. It received the official approval of the Vatican in 1950 and was given the privilege of becoming a "personal prelature" of the pope in 1982. This means, in effect, that Opus Dei is its own diocese, much like a military archdiocese, without geographical boundaries, and functions as such within existing dioceses. Even so, its members still remain under the authority of the local bishop.

Opus Dei is clearly not a "sect" in any sense of the word. It has its own rules and practices, much like a religious order and, like any approved religious order, functions entirely within the bounds of Catholic Church law.

84. One of Dan Brown's villains is a "monk" of Opus Dei named Silas. Does Opus Dei have monks?

No. Opus Dei is not a religious *order* in the traditional sense of the word. In traditional religious orders, such as Benedictines or Dominicans, men and women separate themselves from the world in order to pursue a more intense relationship with God. The members of Opus Dei remain in the world and carry out the normal tasks of careers and family life. Thus, it is more accurate to call Opus Dei a "secular institute," which is not a religious order as such, but an organization whose members consecrate themselves to God while continuing to live in the "secular" state, or the world. While members of Opus Dei do not take vows, some members choose celibacy as a sign of a more complete commitment. These are called "numeraries" and live in small communities. Unlike Dan Brown's Opus Dei "monk" Silas, members of Opus Dei do not wear religious robes or habits. Opus Dei members are encouraged to practice some kind of mortification or self-denial, usually involving food and drink. Members might also practice self-flagellation with a small cord, but it is neither required of them nor is it carried to the extreme displayed by Silas, who flogs himself mercilessly.

85. Who is the Silas in the Bible (Acts 16) after whom Dan Brown claims his Opus Dei "monk" is named? Does the Bible really say that Noah was an albino, like Brown's monk Silas?

The story of Silas appears in the Acts of the Apostles, beginning in chapter 15. The early church was faced with a dilemma about Gentile converts and whether they should be held to observance of Jewish laws, and specifically, whether they should be required to be circumcised. After discussing this issue, the church at Jerusalem sent men to the Christian community at Antioch with Paul and Barnabas who were to deliver the letter setting out their decision. This meeting at Jerusalem was the first Church Council and its decision was momentous for the future of the church. One of the men sent was Silas. Silas and his companion, Judas Barsabbas, were called "leaders among the brothers" (Acts 15:22). When they came to Antioch, they "said much to encourage and strengthen the believers" (15:32). After that, Silas accompanied Paul on a tour of the Christian communities in Syria and elsewhere.

In Philippi occurred the event to which Brown refers. Paul drove a spirit of divination out of a slave girl whose owners were making good money from her fortune-telling. Now deprived of their source of income, the girl's owners dragged Paul and Silas before the magistrates and accused them of causing a disturbance, whereupon the authorities had them severely flogged and thrown into prison. While Paul and Silas were praying and singing hymns around midnight, a violent earthquake occurred that shook the prison's foundations and caused all the prisoners' chains to be unfastened. The jailer, waking up and assuming that the prisoners had escaped, went to kill himself with his sword but was stopped by Paul, who assured him that they were still there. Falling down before Paul and Silas, the jailer asked what he must do to be saved. They assured him that he and his household would be saved if he believed in Jesus. They preached the word of God to the jailer and his family, and all were "baptized without delay" (Acts 16:33).

It is this episode that Brown is interested in, because the character Silas in his youth escapes from a prison in Andorra that is destroyed in an earthquake, and thus he gets his name (p. 58).

Brown has Bishop Aringarosa, the Opus Dei prelate, tell Silas that Noah was an albino, saying that Noah had white skin like an angel (pp. 166–67), but Silas hadn't heard this before. This is not surprising, since the Bible doesn't mention it at all. Brown might have been thinking of Moses, whose face would shine when he came down from Mount Sinai after speaking with God (cf. Exod 34:29–36), but he has transferred it to Noah, who, he says, saved all life on earth (by building the ark and taking the creatures into it when the flood came), and he wants to draw a parallel with Silas, who is being called to great deeds.

86. Can Opus Dei be justly accused of secrecy, as Dan Brown implies repeatedly in the book?

In many ways, this is the Achilles heel of Opus Dei. Secrecy was certainly a survival technique in its early days leading up to the Spanish Civil War, when twelve bishops and as many as 8,000 priests and religious were put to death, but such methods do not sit well in a free society. While every organization has its own methods of recruitment and formation, Opus Dei continues to be more secretive than most. Dan Brown is certainly irresponsible in his accusations about Opus Dei, and hides behind the veil of his book being a "novel," but such irresponsibility results partly from the secrecy with which Opus Dei continues to function.

ELEVEN

THE JEWISH TRADITION

87. After flagellating himself, Silas prays, "Purge me with hyssop and I shall be clean," while washing away the blood (p. 31). Supposedly he is quoting from the Book of Psalms. Are these the same psalms that we pray at Mass in the Responsorial Psalm?

Yes. This quote prayed by Silas is from Psalm 51, the greatest of the "penitential psalms, which begins, "Have mercy on me, O God, according to your steadfast love." Brown is so intent upon accusing the Catholic Church of persecuting paganism in order to advance its own agenda that he consistently ignores Christianity's evolution from Jewish roots. Jesus, his family and friends, his disciples, and the earliest Christians were devout Jews. This meant that the earliest Christian prayers came from the Jewish prayer tradition, the backbone of which is the 150 psalms in the biblical Book of Psalms.

Although we often associate King David with the psalms, he did not compose them all; in fact, many of the psalms were quite obviously composed several hundred years after David lived. But he did encourage the writing of psalms and the gathering of their texts into collections. The Book of Psalms as it now exists is actually a collection of five smaller books of psalms.

88. So, our Catholic liturgy has adopted the psalms from the Hebrew Scriptures?

Yes. The psalm we're most frequently aware of is the Responsorial Psalm, which follows the first reading at every Mass. Often a part rather than an entire psalm is used here; the Responsorial Psalm should reflect the mood or theme of the reading we've just heard, and so the verses that don't contribute to this may be left out.

The psalms also have a very prominent place in the Liturgy of the Hours, or what used to be called the Divine Office. The Liturgy of the Hours, formerly thought of as the exclusive property of the clergy, is increasingly prayed by lay Catholics in groups and privately, and more and more Catholics are using psalms in other forms of personal prayer. The psalms have words for any situation or feeling you can think of, whether positive, negative, or in between, and large numbers of Catholics have been discovering and enjoying this rich treasury of prayers ever since Pope Paul VI moved to begin popularizing the Liturgy of the Hours among the laity. This is what's important about the psalms, not whether they're a suitable accompaniment to the oddball practices of a fictitious "monk" (see Q. 84).

89. No doubt there are many other psalm texts we're familiar with and don't even realize that they're from the Book of Psalms. Can you mention any?

One of the best places to look is in the accounts of Jesus' passion in the four Gospels. In Matthew's Gospel, shortly before Jesus dies he cries out, "My God, my God, why have you forsaken me?" (27:46). This is the opening line of Psalm 22, which is known and beloved as a great "passion psalm" because of all the references to it in the four passion accounts. The idea of the soldiers casting lots to divide up the clothing of the crucified Jesus; the people mocking Jesus and challenging him to come down from the cross if he is the Son of God and trusts in God— these are both allusions to Psalm 22. It was important for the early Christians to know that Jesus was the fulfillment of the prophecies in the Hebrew Scriptures, and they would have recognized these allusions.

After the resurrection, Luke tells us, Jesus met two disciples on the road to Emmaus and, "beginning with Moses and all the prophets, he interpreted to them the things about himself in all the scriptures" (24:27)—among which were, of course, the psalms.

In Luke's Gospel Jesus' last words are, "Father, into your hands I commend my spirit" (23:46), words taken from Psalm 31. We do well to remember that in both Psalm 22 and Psalm 31 the psalmist is in deep distress and yet expresses steadfast trust in God. If we apply this to Jesus, we realize that in his darkest moments—and what could be darker than having your friends run away while you are crucified as a criminal?—Jesus, deep down, never lost trust in God, and because of this, God raised him up again.

If your Bible lists cross-references to similar passages elsewhere in the Bible—usually you will find this at the bottom of each page, or perhaps in a box or sidebar—you will be able to look in the Gospels and other New Testament writings and locate many allusions to or quotes from the psalms. The awesome Letter to the Hebrews is a particularly rich source. And did you know that Mary's *Magnificat* (Luke 1:46–55) is actually a psalm?

90. During his search for the Grail, Silas finds a stone tablet in the floor of the Church of Saint-Sulpice in Paris (pp. 127–29). He lifts it out and discovers that it has an inscription—Job 38:11. The text of this verse, which Silas looks up in a Bible on the altar, reads, "Hitherto shalt thou come, but no further." It sounds as if this is meant to apply to Silas's quest for the Grail. What does the verse really mean?

Brown is quite correct in describing Job as someone whose faith survived repeated trials (p. 128). But the quoted verse—Job 38:11—has a very different meaning in its original context from the interpretation Brown gives it.

The Book of Job belongs to the genre of wisdom literature; that is, unlike other books of the Hebrew Scriptures that deal with salvation history, wisdom literature is concerned chiefly with philosophical questions about life and death as they affect people universally, and not only the chosen people of God. Unknown to Job, God is allowing Satan to test him to see whether an unrelenting series of setbacks will put a dent in Job's steadfast faith.

Throughout the book, in discourse with his three friends, Job maintains his innocence, insisting that he is a righteous man who has done nothing to deserve this incredible suffering. Job is right and God, Job declares, is wrong.

At a dramatic moment in the conversation God himself breaks in, not offering answers to Job's "Why me?" questions but, instead, posing new questions of his own. Who is Job to question God? Can Job view all things from the vantage point of the infinitely wise Creator? God's power and wisdom are beyond what humans can comprehend, and God recites, in a series of eloquent rhetorical questions, the myriad ways in which he has ordered creation.

Here, then, is Brown's quotation restored to its original context in God's speech:

> "...who shut in the sea with doors
>   When I burst out from the womb?—
> when I...prescribed bounds for it,...
> and said, 'thus far shall you come,
>   and no farther...'?" (38:8, 10, 11)

God is saying that, as immense, powerful, and seemingly limitless as the sea is, God is still more powerful, for it is God who has set the boundaries for the sea. In ancient Hebrew literature the sea was an important symbol of elemental might, and this reference to God's still greater power occurs more than once in the scriptures.

91. Who is Shekinah? Brown refers to her as a powerful female equal of God (p. 309).

Shekinah has various meanings, the most common of which signifies the dwelling or presence of God among the people, the manifestation of God in the world. It may seem paradoxical to us, but this word that indicated the immanence of God (God's nearness in the world) was also used as a substitute for God's name in contexts that might otherwise suggest an anthropomorphic view of God — that is, might equate God with human beings. Thus, *Shekinah* also helped safeguard the divine transcendence.

The word *Shekinah* first appears in early postbiblical texts such as the Talmud (interpretations of the Mishna or codification of Jewish oral laws), Midrash (interpretations of scripture that derive from oral tradition), and Targumim (interpretive Aramaic translations of the Hebrew Scriptures). Not until later — in the medieval period and beyond — did some Jewish philosophers begin thinking of the Shekinah as something distinct from God, and the notion of the Shekinah as a feminine principle only originated with the Kabbalists in medieval or early modern times.

Thus Brown's suggestion that "early Jews" — he obviously means Jews who lived several centuries before the Christian era began — believed that the Shekinah (which is *not* a personal name) resided in Solomon's Temple is both anachronistic and erroneous, as is the notion that Jews at this time conceived of the Shekinah as a female deity. The term was not even in use then.

Interestingly, some commentators point out certain affinities between the concept of Shekinah and the Holy Spirit.

92. Does this mean, then, that the Star of David has nothing to do with the dwelling-place of male (Yahweh) and female (Shekinah) deities, as Brown suggests (p. 446)?

The symbol we now know as the Star of David quite likely originated as a magical symbol, and was possibly even thought of by the Kabbalists as having the power to ward off evil spirits, but the idea that it has anything to do with Yahweh and Shekinah is erroneous, because, as we've noted (see Q. 95), neither the actual concept of Shekinah nor the notion of the Shekinah as the female principle is particularly ancient.

Although it dates from antiquity, the Star of David — in Hebrew called *Magen David* or "Shield of David" — did not originate as an exclusively Jewish symbol; in fact, it appeared on some medieval cathedrals. Its use within Judaism really began to spread from the seventeenth century onward, when the Jews in Prague, in the present-day Czech Republic, adopted it in an official sense. By the nineteenth century the Jewish people had almost universally adopted the Star of David; it serves, one could say, as a symbolic counterpart to the cross in Christianity.

93. Were sacred rituals involving sex with priestesses ever part of early Jewish worship, as Brown says (p. 309)?

Never. There were times when the Israelites strayed from worship of Yahweh, their one true God, and instead fell into the cults of the pagan gods of the non-Jewish nations among whom they lived. Undoubtedly such pagan worship did involve "sacred prostitution" and was carried out within the very precincts of the Temple, but this was an aberration and never part of the Jewish religion. Time and again courageous prophets, such as Jeremiah, appeared and berated the people for succumbing to these licentious ways. Time and again the people repented and returned to Yahweh, the true God. Time and again Yahweh took them back so that, through it all, they remained his special people. In the overall history of the chosen people, it is this steadfast faithfulness of God, God's constant willingness to forgive his sinful people, that's important—that constitutes an unbroken thread running through the fabric of salvation history—and not some sensational pseudo-secret about experiencing the divine through sexual union with priestesses.

94. Where does "Yahweh," the personal name of Israel's God, come from?

Brown gives a totally false account of the origin of the name Yahweh (p. 309). In the Bible we first meet the name in Exodus, in the story of Moses and the burning bush in which God reveals himself to Moses. When Moses asks God's name, God replies, "I am who am." This is the closest we get in English to a translation of the word we say as "Yahweh." It means something like "he who is," and it comes from the Hebrew verb *hawah,* which means "to be." As Roland Faley points out, "God is identified with the verb 'to be' because *he is the God who is as opposed to the gods who are not....this is the God who really is*" (*From Genesis to Apocalypse,* p. 80). Recall that in the Gospels Jesus infuriates the Jewish leaders by saying of himself, "I am" (John 8:58). The identification with the God of Israel was unmistakable.

Thus the roots of "Yahweh" have nothing whatever to do with an androgynous union between the masculine *Jah* and *Hawah,* meaning "Eve," as Brown states. (The Hebrews never came near to equating Eve with a deity!) In fact, he gets the relationship between "Yahweh" and "Jehovah" completely backward by claiming that YHWH derived from Jehovah. The opposite is true. God's name was held to be so sacred that it was never pronounced or written, and so it was spelled YHWH because the vowels were left out in writing. People pronounced the alternative names for God, Adonai or Elohim, when they came to YHWH in the text. Later scholars producing written editions of the scriptures filled in the vowels of one of these alternative names between the consonants YHWH, and thus the artificial name "Jehovah" was born—a name with no greater antiquity than the medieval period, less than one thousand years ago! It gained currency in English when it was widely used by Christian scholars during the Renaissance and Reformation era for translations of the Bible, notably the King James Version. More recent research indicated that "Yahweh" had originally been the correct pronunciation of the name, and it became more frequently used when it was taken up by biblical scholars in the nineteenth and twentieth centuries.

TWELVE

LEONARDO DA VINCI

95. *The Da Vinci Code* **centers on the supposed activities of a real artist. What are the basic outlines of the life of Leonardo da Vinci?**

Leonardo was born in 1452 at his father's estate in Vinci, a small Tuscan village in the region of Florence, Italy. Thus "da Vinci" simply means "from Vinci," indicating where the artist was from, and Brown errs by consistently calling him "Da Vinci" as if it were the artist's last name—much as people often wrongly assume that "von Bingen" is part of Hildegard's name instead of a reference to the place with which she is closely associated.

Leonardo's artistic gifts were evident early, and at age fifteen his father apprenticed him to the well-known artist Andrea del Verrocchio. Leonardo's earliest known works are his contributions to paintings executed in Verrocchio's workshop, including a *Baptism of Christ* and two *Annunciations*. His exquisitely sorrowful *St. Jerome* and the *Adoration of the Magi* also date from this period.

In 1482 Leonardo moved to Milan, where he spent seventeen years in the service of the duke. Here his skills and talents blossomed in all directions, so that he achieved a reputation not only as an artist but also as technical adviser in architecture and engineering. It was at this time that he began keeping his famous notebooks. He also established a workshop with apprentices and students. The two versions of *Virgin of the Rocks* (which Brown misnames *Madonna*) were painted here, as was *The Last Supper*.

After Leonardo left Milan he lived and worked in and around Florence (1500–1506), where he painted the famous *Virgin and Child with St. Anne* and *Mona Lisa* and engaged in intensive scientific studies. He returned to Milan in 1506–13, then went to Rome, and in 1516 he left Italy forever to enter the service of King Francis I of France, where he died in 1519.

96. *The Da Vinci Code* **portrays its eponymous hero as involved in all sorts of arcane and esoteric activities. How much of it is true? And was Leonardo a flamboyant homosexual, as Brown claims?**

Actually, none of those claims is true. Leonardo was an intensely practical man whose interest in science rivaled his interest in art; in fact, the two served and enhanced each other. He filled vast quantities of notebooks with scientific sketches and plans and the results of his observations and experiments. These notebooks filled literally thousands of pages with writings and sketches. His famous plans for a "flying machine" were based not on any notions of UFOs (if one wants to descend to the level of Picknett and Prince and Teabing's other "sources," see Q. 1) but on sound scientific principles and close observation of the flight of birds. His extensively detailed plan—complete with diagrams and a map—to build a canal that would connect Florence to the sea was never realized, but when the express highway between Florence and the sea was built in recent times, it took the exact route Leonardo had chosen for the canal. He was a recognized expert in hydraulic engineering.

At age thirty Leonardo gave up a promising career in his native Florence to work in Milan, likely because he preferred Milan's realistic academic atmosphere to the Neoplatonism of Florence. This hardly adds up to a picture of someone who would spend time getting heavily involved in anything as esoteric as the Priory of Sion, had such an organization even existed at the time.

Unlike Michelangelo, who was known to be homosexual, Leonardo has left no explicit indications about his sexuality. He was a very private person who reveals precious little about himself in his writings. What we do know from his notebooks is that he didn't appear interested in sex; he was a lonely man who sublimated all his energies into his prodigious work, and he prioritized and valued the intellectual life above sensual concerns.

Author Sherwin Nuland, in *Leonardo da Vinci*, has discovered an incident in Leonardo's youth in which he was accused, along with three other youths, of sodomizing a male prostitute. The charges were dropped for lack of evidence.

During his second period in Milan (1506–13), Leonardo formed a friendship with one of his apprentices, a young nobleman named Francesco Melzi. Melzi became a faithful and devoted companion who accompanied Leonardo when he left Italy for France, and he remained with him until his death. To Melzi Leonardo bequeathed all his papers. Leonardo's famous treatise on painting was, in fact, lovingly compiled and arranged by Melzi from Leonardo's writings. Whether this relationship would have qualified as homosexual, there is no evidence to indicate either way. It appears quite obvious, however, that if Leonardo *was* gay, he certainly was not "flamboyant."

97. Leonardo seems to have painted many works with religious themes. Can it be true, then, that he was contemptuous of religion and especially of the Catholic Church?

Leonardo's notebooks don't reveal anything of the kind. Like many enlightened people of his time, he seems to have objected to abuses, such as indulgences, that eventually led to the Protestant Reformation (he lived a generation before Martin Luther and died two years after Luther posted his famous "95 Theses"). The two quotes by him in *The Da Vinci Code* (p. 231) are completely lifted out of their original contexts and, despite what Teabing says, do not refer to the Bible. One, about "deceiving the foolish multitude," actually refers to alchemy, while the other, exhorting "wretched mortals" to "open [their] eyes," criticizes ignorance in general.

98. What about *The Last Supper*—is Brown correct in his assertion that the figure next to Jesus is not the apostle John but Mary Magdalene? And what about the painting's hidden connection with the Grail?

Considering that *The Last Supper* is probably the most intensely studied painting in the history of Western art, how is it that no art historian before the fictitious Leigh Teabing ever noticed that the apostle John in the painting is really a woman? For one thing, it makes no sense that Leonardo would include all of the apostles except Christ's favorite, John—especially since this "beloved disciple" is the one from whom the Gospel of John, on which the painting is based, originated (see Q. 12). Further, if the supposed figure of St. John really were a woman, why would it not be Mary, the mother of Jesus, who is mentioned in the Gospel of John as present at the crucifixion and has been depicted in pious paintings as presiding over the apostles after the crucifixion?

The fact is that painters of the Italian Renaissance often portrayed young men as androgynous or feminine. Leonardo's own *John the Baptist* is a case in point, as are paintings by Raphael, including his own self-portraits.

For a connection with the Grail even to begin to be possible, the painting would have to be depicting Jesus instituting the Eucharist. However, Leonardo's depiction of the Last Supper focuses not on the institution of the Eucharist, but on the prediction that Judas would betray him. This was a favorite theme among Renaissance painters, and it was based on the account of the Last Supper in the Gospel of John, which does not contain the story of the institution of the Eucharist. The contrast between the agitated disciples and the serene Jesus faithfully evokes John's Gospel, in which Jesus remains totally in control of his fate and goes to his death as to his hour of glory. To use Leonardo's painting as a meditation on Christ's passion as recounted in John's Gospel is surely more faithful to the artist's intention than to dredge up so much esoteric nonsense about it.

99. What is the meaning of the dagger that St. Peter is holding in the picture? Is he really threatening someone with it?

Leonardo's notebooks refer to the apostle "holding a *knife* [not a dagger] in one hand and in the other the bread divided by this knife" (Edward MacCurdy, ed. and trans., *The Notebooks of*

Leonardo da Vinci, p. 1015). Obviously the artist intended the knife as a mere utilitarian tool for slicing the bread! Possibly the knife may also allude to Peter's later cutting off the ear of one of the soldiers in the garden of Gethsemane, although the Gospel of St. John speaks of a sword rather than a knife.

100. Is Dan Brown correct in claiming that Leonardo deviously used the *Mona Lisa* to hide messages subversive to the church?

It is highly doubtful that Leonardo would recognize any of the meanings read into the *Mona Lisa* by Dan Brown, who calls it "one of the world's most documented inside jokes" (p. 119). Brown contends that the figure in this painting is really a man, and possibly Leonardo himself in drag. He supports this rather confusedly by pointing out that the face of the woman in the painting is turned slightly, highlighting and enlarging her left (or female) side. This is usually called "perspective" in artistic circles and was a growing practice among portrait artists at the time. Leonardo had earlier painted another woman's portrait, the *Lady with an Ermine,* using the same turning technique, although in her case her right (masculine?) side is highlighted.

Brown also makes a bizarre connection between the *Mona Lisa* and an Egyptian god of masculinity named "Amon" and his supposed counterpart, the Egyptian goddess Isis, or "L'Isa"; Brown then "reveals" that an anagram of the two names is "Mona Lisa," making it a divine union of male and female (p. 121). The difficulties with this are twofold. First, the male counterpart of Isis was not Amon, a sun god, but Osiris, whose testicles are still said to reside in the Nile River and are thus a source of fertility for the region. An even more imposing difficulty for Brown is that Leonardo did not call his painting *Mona Lisa* but *La Gioconda,* after the woman in the painting—the wife of Francesco del Giocondo. The earliest known reference to this painting as *Mona*

Lisa is in Giorgio Vasari's biography of Leonardo, written about thirty years after Leonardo had died.

101. Brown gives some technical information about the execution of Leonardo's paintings. Is his information correct?

Not really. *The Last Supper* is *not* a fresco, as Dan Brown claims; frescoes were very difficult to execute (water-based pigments on moistened lime plaster), and even some of the greatest Renaissance painters had terrible problems with the medium. Leonardo was one of them. Even Michelangelo, as Ross King's book *Michelangelo and the Pope's Ceiling* dramatically points out, was a curious choice to execute the ceiling of the Sistine Chapel, since until then he did not seem to have a good grasp of the difficult mechanics of fresco painting; he had failed at previous attempts and regarded himself primarily as a sculptor. Leonardo tried to avoid the fresco process altogether in his *Last Supper* and simply applied tempura onto a thin plaster base. It did not work as the paint did not adhere, and the painting has been in a miserable condition ever since. So little hope was there of preserving the painting that a Dominican prior had a door put through the wall on which *The Last Supper* hung.

Further, Leonardo's painting in the Louvre, the *Virgin of the Rocks* (which Brown incorrectly calls *Madonna of the Rocks*), was not commissioned by a group of nuns, as Brown claims (p. 138), but by a confraternity of men called the Confraternity of the Immaculate Conception, devoted to promoting the veneration of Mary's Immaculate Conception. There are two versions of this painting, one in the National Gallery of London and the other in the Louvre. Brown describes the one in the Louvre, with which the book is directly concerned, as a "five-foot tall canvas" (p. 133). It is actually about six and a half feet high and about four feet across and is set on wood (not canvas) and in a heavy wooden frame. It would have been a superhuman feat for the petite Sophie to pull this down from the wall and walk around the gallery with it, as she does in the book.

Finally, Leonardo did not get "hundreds of lucrative Vatican commissions" (p. 45), but only one, for a painting of *Leda and the Swan*!

Coda

A Final Question

Q. How did *The Da Vinci Code*, with its preposterous historical claims and its hypocritically condescending attitude toward women, achieve such phenomenal success? And what can the average person do in the face of the novel's claims about Catholicism?

Leaving aside the distorted history and the undercurrent of sexism, we have the claims of most readers that *The Da Vinci Code* is a "page-turner," that the chase is exciting and the puzzle intriguing. The supposed exposé also adds to the excitement—we are not only trying to solve this particular crime, we are also gleaning clues to the "true identity" of a church that actually exists.

But in reality, we *can't* leave the distortions and inaccuracies aside. It seems to be all too true that anti-Catholicism is one of the last acceptable prejudices in our politically correct world. The timing of *The Da Vinci Code*'s release was fortuitous (for the author, that is), coinciding as it did with the aftermath of the first outbreaks of news about the sexual abuse scandals. The novel's negative attitude toward the Catholic Church put what photographers call a polarizing filter on the critical lens through which society at large was then regarding the church.

We should never underestimate the power of the written word—even a novel—to influence the individual, or society at large, for good or for ill. With the rise of the Internet and such media forms as sports entertainment and even, it seems, news entertainment, the line between fact and fiction has become increasingly blurred so that it can be difficult to distinguish between them.

It is important to be informed. There is no better defense against falsehood and distortion than the truth. Know what constitutes a good historian. Learn to recognize authentic historical

141

fiction. Know the history of the church and become well acquainted with our ancestors in the faith; they are, after all, our family!

We hope that this book has helped in that process.

SUGGESTED READING

Barber, Richard. *The Holy Grail: Imagination and Belief.* Cambridge, MA: Harvard University Press, 2004.

Brown, Raymond. *An Introduction to New Testament Christology.* New York/Mahwah: Paulist Press, 1994.

Faley, Roland J., TOR. *From Genesis to Apocalypse: Introducing the Bible.* New York/Mahwah: Paulist Press, 1995.

de Flon, Nancy Marie. *The Joy of Praying the Psalms.* Totowa, NJ: Resurrection Press, 2005.

Hearon, Holly E. *The Mary Magdalene Tradition: Witness and Counter-Witness in Early Christian Communities.* Collegeville, MN: Liturgical Press, 2004.

Malone, Mary T. *Women and Christianity.* Vol. 1, *The First Thousand Years.* Vol. 2, *From 1000 to the Reformation.* Vol. 3, *From the Reformation to the 21st Century.* Maryknoll, NY: Orbis Books, 2001, 2002, 2003.

Martin, James J., SJ. "Opus Dei in the United States." *America* (February 25, 1995). www.americamagazine.org/articles/martin-opusdei.cfm

Parker, William J., CSsR. "The Gospels the Church Left Behind." *Liguorian* (July-August 2004): 10–13.

The Psalms: New Catholic Version. Totowa, NJ: Catholic Book Publishing Company, 2002.

Opus Dei Web site. http://*www.opusdei.org*.

Thompson, Mary. *Mary of Magdala: What* The Da Vinci Code *Misses*. New York/Mahwah: Paulist Press, 2006.

Vallée, Gérard. *The Shaping of Christianity: The History and Literature of Its Formative Centuries (100–800)*. New York/Mahwah: Paulist Press, 1999.

Vidmar, John, OP. *The Catholic Church Through the Ages: A History*. New York/Mahwah: Paulist Press, 2005.

"Women Officeholders in the Early Church." Based on the work of Ute Eisen and Dorothy Irvin. Available from the Web site of FutureChurch. http://www.futurechurch.org.